This devotional book is a gentle, clear, and encouraging companion for anyone who wants to know Jesus better—and follow him more fully. No matter where your calling might take you, these daily reflections offer a meaningful way to begin a conversation with the Lord. This book is a treasure for all believers. It's perfect whether you're praying for or supporting missionaries, raising children, or seeking to live out your own unique calling. The timeless truths shared here apply to everyone. Enjoy!

Pam Arlund, PhD
Editor, *Perspectives on the World Christian Movement, 5th Ed*
Director of Training, All Nations International

I warmly recommend this book—not for a quick read, but for quiet reflection. Whether "sender" or "sent," walk a bit with Daniels as you read words written from his heart and from years of living out the vision and calling he has received from God.

David Greenlee, PhD
International Research Associate, Operation Mobilization

With colorful and captivating prose, my longtime missions colleague Gene has captured the mindset of those devoted to missions—both those who never set foot on "the field" and those who make it their home. He truly "gets it," expressing with refreshing honesty and clarity the places I've been.

Becky Watt
Co-founder, Reaching Unreached Nations (RUN) Ministries

Meditations for the Missions Heart

A 40-Day Journey to *Renew* Your Vision

GENE DANIELS

Meditations for the Missions Heart: A 40-Day Journey to Renew Your Vision

Previously published by Condeo Press in 2012, but out of print since 2022.

Published by William Carey Publishing
10 W. Dry Creek Cir
Littleton, CO 80120 | www.missionbooks.org

William Carey Publishing is a ministry of Frontier Ventures
Pasadena, CA | www.frontierventures.org
Cover and Interior Designer: Mike Riester

ISBNs: 978-1-64508-677-2 (paperback)
978-1-64508-678–9 (epub)

Printed Worldwide

29 28 27 26 25 1 2 3 4 5 IN

Library of Congress Control Number: 2025942074

Contents

The Journey Begins

I have a good friend who lives on the West Coast; we have known each other for more than a decade. The funny thing is, we have only actually seen each other one or two times. The problem is, I have spent most of these years physically living in Central Asia, but for my friend, it's only her heart that lives in that faraway place of steppe and high mountain passes.

Though she has only once visited the peoples of the ancient Silk Road, this saint spends hours on her face before God, asking for their souls. She does this because she has seen something of the eternal off in the distance, and it has changed her life's priorities. Yet this vision has also caused her a great deal of discouragement and misunderstanding because most of her brothers and sisters in Christendom do not understand the things that stir her soul.

For me, it's easy. For many years I lived and spoke of Jesus in a foreign land; therefore, I am a missionary. But what do you call my friend? A "support person?" Not quite right. A "missions mobilizer?" Not really. "Absolutely essential" would be closer to the truth, although she really doesn't fit into any of the boxes that we have so neatly drawn around the concept of world missions.

I have another good friend—actually, she's more like a big sister. I have learned a lot from her over the years, mostly about sacrifice and perseverance. She has taught me these lessons because she has poured out her entire adult life in hard and difficult places—places where people have never heard the name of Jesus.

This big sister of mine spends hours and hours in dirty bazaars and other grimy places, anywhere she might find precious souls to be snatched from the fire. She considers no soil off-limits to her evangelistic calling, but her roots have grown deep in strange and challenging fields—places most people would be unwilling to visit, much less live.

Like my first friend, she also does such things because years ago she saw something of the eternal off in the distance, and it changed her life's priorities. Unfortunately, these are priorities that few understand and even fewer share.

What is the burden these two women have in common? What is it that causes each of them, in their own way, to face the uphill struggle they have chosen as a way of life? What kind of burden can be stronger and more real than the empty stare of family and friends who don't seem to get it?

The best way I can describe this passion is to call it a "missions heart." It is a heart that has been deeply touched by something so far off in the distance that most others won't ever see it. And this encounter changes our life priorities. This is a soul who has heard the voice of eternity crying out to faraway peoples who have yet to hear the great shepherd's voice.

I understand the wrestling that goes on in both missions hearts. At different points in my own journey, I have lived in both of their worlds.

For years, I was sure of a calling to the ends of the earth but found no outlet other than on my knees. I've felt that sense of being "out of place," which gnaws at those who stay home yet live every day thinking about the nations.

In retrospect, I can see that what felt like forever was, in fact, only a season that God used to fill my heart with his passion. It was a time through which he taught me how to struggle with one of life's many paradoxes.

Then, for several years, I had the privilege of serving the Lord in some of those places of which I used to only dream. But I have also found that those glorious daydreams can morph into nightmares of discouragement—floodwaters that leave muddy stains on your heart. And just as before, God had to teach me to live out his purposes in my life and family, even when it involves the realities of living far from our homeland.

Through these experiences, I have come to appreciate an important truth. There is a missions heart that gives itself away in unknown places with unpronounceable names. And there is also a missions heart, just as sure, just as unknown, that cries out to God in full view of a church on every corner. The heart-level struggles of these two are very much the same; only their roles in the kingdom differ. Both make sacrifices in a silent war that most of the Christian world seems to know nothing about. They both must wage a daily battle to maintain vision; only by listening with their hearts can they press on.

So, it is to strengthen these people, these missions hearts, that I have written the following devotions. Some of these thoughts will perhaps speak more to the one who is struggling on the home front, while others may speak more deeply to those facing the discouragement of life in foreign lands. Nevertheless, the need of both to nourish their souls' passion is quite similar.

If you are now carrying God's burden for the nations, regardless of what your role might be, my hope is that this little book will refresh you. If in the past, you felt such a stirring but have given up your zeal for lesser pursuits, my desire is that by the time you finish these few pages, something will have rekindled your God-given flame.

However, be forewarned. If you have never felt the urge to cry over a world map, it is doubtful the following thoughts will make much sense to you. So, to my praying friend on the West Coast, and to my big sister living in yet another awful location—I offer these words of encouragement so you will remain in the battle.

How to Use This Devotional

Whenever someone picks up a short book like this one, it is tempting to read it straight through, and that would not be the worst way to spend a quiet afternoon. However, to get the most out of these Scripture meditations, I suggest you use it the way it was designed—as a forty-day devotional. This way, each day's reading can encourage you from a slightly different angle in the light of a new day.

Also, by following the forty-day plan, you allow some time between readings for the Holy Spirit to weave them together and connect them with the good things already in your heart. So, although each reading stands independent of the others, I pray that they will be like a path toward a stronger, renewed place in your spiritual life.

I should, however, comment that there is nothing magical about forty days, although it does have a certain biblical ring to it. The main reason I chose this format is that it fits well with my vision for this book: to offer my readers a short, intense reminder of the glorious vision that first caused them to become involved with world mission. So rather than waxing long now, I bid you adieu and trust that the Lord will meet you in the following pages.

1 Our Common Struggle

I urge you, brothers and sisters,
by our Lord Jesus Christ and by the love of the Spirit,
to join me in my struggle by praying to God for me.
—Romans 15:30

Paul was writing back from the front lines of a spiritual war, asking the Christians in Rome to "join" him in his struggle. But in the days of donkey and camel travel, just how did he expect them to do this from hundreds of miles away?

Times have certainly changed. We have internet phone service and video conferencing, but the question remains: How do we truly join hands together across the world in mission? What does it look like in the spiritual realm when those on the field and those at home partner to fulfill the Great Commission? Perhaps we should begin by trying to understand the concept of spiritual position.

With a world map in hand, we can quickly identify the exact geographic location of a missionary living in a hostile foreign country for the sake of the gospel. The physical arena of their calling defines their position. But what of the missions hearts back home? What is their position on the spiritual map of world missions?

First, we must understand that in the kingdom of God, spiritual position means much more than the place where one happens to be drawing breath. The most important question is not, "In what city do you dress for work most mornings?" but rather, "Where is your heart beating while in prayer?"

There are some good and decent missionaries in faraway foreign fields who live as if their hearts are back home on a couch watching TV. There are also people who will always live in the same small hometown yet suffer and bleed with those on the gospel frontiers as if they were there in the flesh. The distance is nothing to them because they can literally see the lost of the nations with their hearts. The truth is, the position of the heart is all that really matters.

There is a great need for more people at home who clearly understand this truth: unsung heroes who realize that their assigned place of service is on their faces before God.

This is implied by Paul's words here near the end of Romans. He asked his friends to "join" him, but I do not think he expected them to make a trip. To Paul, the moment they hit their knees in Rome, they joined him in resistance against an unseen enemy circling over his head in Corinth. Their hearts immediately moved them from beside their bed or mat to the front lines, by divine calling, taking their solemn place alongside the apostle as he struggled for the faith.

Sometimes I fear that we do not recognize this for the urgent appeal it is. Paul was facing a bona fide war; he was not just writing in metaphor. There were tangible powers of darkness holding captive the people Paul was trying to reach, real demons behind false gods. His preaching had stirred the hatred of a pantheon of Roman deities, and without difficulty, they could find human fists ready for use against the aged apostle.

Paul was in hand-to-hand combat with an unseen enemy, and he needed people who would join their hearts to his, bringing him real aid in a real war. Thankfully, Paul knew where to turn when calling fellow soldiers to join him on the front lines. Evidently, in Rome there were proven men and women who were known to be ready whenever there was a spiritual firefight. Paul didn't have to coerce them. He simply needed to inform them—the time had come; the enemy was now engaged. These were not passive observers of mission; they were able fellow soldiers willing to add the weight and authority of their spiritual calling to the cause.

The huge distinction we usually make between the missionaries on the field and those back home does not exist at this moment on the battlefield. The issue is always one of the heart. There is a great need for more people at home who clearly understand this truth: unsung heroes who realize that their assigned place of service is on their faces before God.

Moreover, no matter what our role in the Great Commission, we must constantly challenge ourselves about the position of our hearts. This is far more important than the physical location of our bodies. In the kingdom of God, there is no such thing as a second-class soldier because of where one physically lives. And that, dear ones, is the beginning of what it means to have a missions heart.

Seeing by the Spirit

"What no eye has seen, what no ear has heard,
and what no human mind has conceived"
—the things God has prepared for those who love him—
these are the things God has revealed to us by his Spirit.
—1 Corinthians 2:9–10

Do we believe this? Do we consider eternal life to hold something so great that our limited human capacities cannot even grasp it now? No, let's make it personal: Do I actually believe this?

The truth is yes, we do—but only sometimes. In our better moments, we set our hearts on another world, but far too often we are rooted in the world that our eyes have seen, our ears have heard, and our minds conceive. This is, predictably, the source of much distress and despair.

The realities of this life can be depressing. And even when they are not, we humans tend to sulk whenever life does not turn out like we hoped. The situation can be all the worse for the missions heart. Besides our own inner struggles, we live acutely aware of the bitter plight suffered by a lost world around us. Together, these can accumulate into a weight that crushes the life out of even the strongest, leaving one spiritually drained and vulnerable. For this reason, some leave their calling, while others continue to serve for decades, but only out of a dreary duty.

If we are to have any joy along our journey, it is vital to learn the secret of daily living in the sunlight from a world beyond. That is why Paul was inspired to lift an Old Testament passage out of Isaiah and then add, "These are the things God has revealed to us by his Spirit." To live in the kingdom of God, without having yet fully received it, we must stay in the Spirit. To transcend this world's bitter siren call, we must constantly tune in to the voice that calls from another realm to the world for which we were born again, our birthright as children of the great King.

We must cultivate an inner ear that is attuned to the love song continuously emanating from the Holy Spirit, drawing us to the Father.

By contrast, our souls become agitated and frustrated when we live within the scope of our natural vision. Our souls see the things we have or don't have—the incomplete or completely lacking pleasures of life. These things stalk the soul and gnaw at the mind when we live without a perpetual view toward eternity.

Therefore, we must cultivate an inner ear that is attuned to the love song continuously emanating from the Holy Spirit, drawing us to the Father. We must learn to recognize the quiet inner voice that draws us toward a future our beloved has gone to prepare—a future that we have yet to see, but which the Spirit himself bears witness to in our hearts.

We must both strive to hear and rest in knowing his voice as it whispers across eternity. These verses call us to see, hear, and know the surpassing greatness of the life awaiting us. We must somehow live in this glow, forever in hope of the glory that has been promised.

Like flowers set on the windowsill in midwinter, we bloom as best we can in the muted light yet live in hope that the full radiance is coming. Yes, beloved, the summer will come. Come quickly, Lord Jesus.

Poor in the Eyes of the World

Listen, my dear brothers and sisters:
Has not God chosen those who are poor in the eyes of the world
to be rich in faith and to inherit the kingdom
he promised those who love him?
—James 2:5

It is not poverty, in the absolute sense, that James refers to here, for poverty is always relative. What is a wealthy, affluent life in one place will be disdained as mere survival in another. As one popular proverb states, one man's trash is another man's treasure.

But James is specifically referring to those who are "poor in the eyes of the world." He is warning us about that green-eyed, envious world around us, whose trends and fads constantly demand more—more of our money, more of our time, more of our hearts. In our materialistic society, it seems any person is poor who is unwilling to live by the motto, "He who has the most toys wins."

Therefore, the eyes of the world mock the missions heart. They look down on the old car or out-of-date clothes that sometimes grace our lives. They sneer about our children being underprivileged because we have chosen to set our hearts on another kingdom.

Nevertheless, this ridicule and the pain that goes along with it comprise a narrow but required passageway that leads from one kingdom to another. Like a surly moneychanger at the international airport, the world's disrespect enables us to exchange the legal tender of this materialistic world for the treasure of a new land.

The currency of the world around us is affluence and wealth, or at least the illusion of such. The coin of the realm to which we are called is entirely different, and to obtain it we must make a willing exchange. Like many things along this journey, this transformation is a mysterious process, shrouded in the working of the Holy Spirit deep within a pilgrim's heart. But somehow, someway, the cold, disapproving stare of a world lusting for mammon becomes God's handmaiden to produce in us faith.

But if we choose to ground our thinking in the wisdom of our Father, we slowly exchange more and more of a wealth that is worthless for our inheritance, which is priceless.

Each time we consciously choose to "seek first his kingdom," we exchange a few coins from one currency to the other. In the beginning, like scared tourists, we change only enough for the day. We fear being taken advantage of as we fumble along with these funny-looking banknotes. At first, the values of this new kingdom feel strange, almost like play money. We are unsure if we can depend on it.

Then, we go into shock when we find out the exchange rate—it is terrible! Most of us have spent many years hoarding up this world's opinion of ourselves. Now we learn that it will buy nothing in this new kingdom. We find that all that we have banked on for years is bankrupt when measured in the land we are called to. For many pilgrims, this is a terrifying transaction, making them long to return to the old system.

But if we choose to ground our thinking in the wisdom of our Father, we slowly exchange more and more of a wealth that is worthless for our inheritance, which is priceless. Now don't misunderstand. We cannot convert our corrupt little nest egg all at once, but coin by coin we buy into a new worldview, into the richness of a new kingdom. Slowly, we send down roots in this strange new place where our status is secured by grace through faith alone. Gradually, almost imperceptibly, we start feeling at home in a land where just knowing the King is of more value than the trinkets of a thousand self-esteem merchants.

If we persevere, we will find, just like our brother James, that to be "poor in the eyes of the world" is a trifling price for the privilege of being "rich in faith."

Waiting for the Morning

Out of the depths I cry to you, LORD; Lord, hear my voice.
Let your ears be attentive to my cry for mercy.
I wait for the Lord more than watchmen wait for
the morning, more than watchmen wait for the morning.
—Psalm 130:1–2, 6

Do these first few verses not sound familiar? How many times have you personally felt that "the depths" were your home, yet hoped and tried to believe that God would still hear you? How many times have you cried for God to be attentive to your prayers?

It must be remembered that David's thoughts at the beginning of the psalm are not complete without those from the end. The first words are misleading until the two are combined because, as a whole, they teach us a pattern of faith-filled living.

The truth is, we all face difficulties and trials, times that feel like we are calling "out of the depths . . ." This is simply part of our human experience. The challenge is to follow through so that these seasons become opportunities to discipline our souls, and to do this, we must teach our souls to wait. But not simply to wait, for everyone does that. Even the whining, impatient child waits, if only for their parent to give in to their tantrum. No, for us, the secret is to wait as "watchmen wait for the morning." So, we must ask, Just how does a watchman wait for the coming of dawn?

The watchman does not simply pass the night, hoping and praying nothing goes wrong; he waits attentively. The watchman strains to listen and peers out into the darkness, trying to adjust his eyes to the night. This is an active, even aggressive, waiting, undertaken with a sense of responsibility. He knows that the lives of the sleeping ones in the city depend on his diligence at the post.

As those who are admired at home and closely scrutinized on the field, the missions heart knows this sense of responsibility. We carry this weight of the watching. It comes with the territory. Therefore, it is important for us to learn to wait well. The people around us expect to see in us an example of one who is spiritually alert, not frantic or asleep at the post.

Further, a watchman is not waiting for just anything to happen; they wait for the morning. The desire of their vigilance is assured. The watchman knows, without any doubt whatsoever, that the sun will rise. They don't fret over the length of the night, even though midwinter's darkness can seem dreadfully long. No, the watchman is not to be deceived by the feelings of the moment; he waits in complete faith that morning will come. He has seen the darkness broken by the dawn many times, so his heart is filled with steadfast anticipation. What he has learned from experience has grown into a conviction.

What has been your experience? Has not God come through for you time and time again? Perhaps not always in the way nor at the time you may have wanted it. But I think we can all testify that his almighty hand is always there, just as the rising of the faithful sun. With such victories as our experience, our waiting should be full of obvious confidence and faith.

Has not God come through for you time and time again?

As weak, failing humans, we seem to be well practiced in the "cry for mercy" part but need much training if we are to learn how to wait as the "watchmen wait for the morning." Yet about this, we need not worry; the one for whom we wait is more concerned about our character than our circumstances. He will arrange many opportunities for us to be taught how to "wait for the morning."

5 A Brother at Arms

Epaphroditus, my brother,
co-worker and fellow soldier . . . welcome him in the Lord
with great joy, and honor people like him.
—Philippians 2:25, 29

Such a testimony—"Welcome him in the Lord with great joy, and honor people like him." Yet, Paul said this concerning a man we barely know anything about! Therefore, even though he only briefly graces the pages of Scripture, we should try to learn all we can about what kind of man he was.

The biographical information on Epaphroditus is slim: He was a church leader from Philippi, he served as what we today call a "short-term" missionary, and he nearly died while carrying money to Paul in Rome. That's it. We really don't know anything else about him, yet he left behind a powerful legacy to challenge us. Whatever he did and however he conducted himself, it impressed the apostle Paul—a man who does not strike me as easily impressed!

What was it about Epaphroditus that made such an impact? Was he a great evangelist? Was he a profound man of prayer? We really don't know. But Paul did paint some short word pictures about the character of this short-term visitor; therefore, it is to those snapshots that we now turn.

"My brother"—Paul often referred to "the brothers" in a general sense, but this is the only time he personalized the term to "my brother." What does this point to? We know Paul was in hard straits at Rome. He was under arrest, facing an unknown fate. Timothy was a man he could count on, but other than him, it seems there was no one else who cared about the things that stirred Paul's apostolic soul. Then Epaphroditus drops in and turns out to be a man of the same blood as Paul himself. They connected at a deep level, and with what we know about Paul, that level was likely a passion for Christ.

Epaphroditus exhibited the same disciplined, hardship-bearing attitude that characterized Paul's life.

"Fellow worker"—Unfortunately, the term worker cannot be honestly used to describe all short-term missionaries today. Too many come to visit the mission field because they want a cross-cultural experience, but this visitor from Philippi was different—he was a worker. Epaphroditus didn't come to Rome to be shown around and do some shopping in the famous bazaars. He was a fellow worker to the veteran missionary because he did not come to the field thinking about what he or the church back home would get out of the trip. He came to serve. And the apostle took note of this. He honored Epaphroditus in this letter because this short-term missionary understood that ministry is a labor of love, but hard labor nonetheless.

"Fellow soldier"—Lastly, Paul was a tough-minded, disciplined man of action. He spent his life waging a personal, intense battle for the souls of men. Therefore, when he calls someone a "fellow soldier," we should consider it perhaps the highest words of honor he would bestow on someone! Epaphroditus exhibited the same disciplined, hardship-bearing attitude that characterized Paul's life. It ministered to Paul's soul to see someone from back home who was just as willing to live and die for the sake of their calling as he was.

In these three brief snapshots, Paul portrayed the character of the short-term missionary Epaphroditus. Paul's words about this man should confront us personally and raise the bar for what we expect of those we serve with in mission. We should challenge one another to aspire to the example of this fine brother from Philippi, an obscure man whose short missions ministry made a lasting impression on the apostle Paul—as it should on us.

As Strangers in This World

Dear friends, I urge you, as foreigners and exiles . . .
—1 Peter 2:11

This is a difficult word picture for most Christians in the Western world to grasp. They cannot imagine the sense of distance and alienation Peter captured here for his first-century audience. Not so for the missions heart. Like a turbaned Muslim cleric at a bar mitzvah, the missions heart is keenly aware of being out of place, that this world is not where we belong.

Those who have lived as foreigners to a foreign culture know the daily grind of feeling like an outsider. We have often felt the helplessness of missing normal cultural cues or staring blankly at other people's jokes. We are accustomed to walking the same sidewalks as the crowds but living with a completely different worldview. Our kids may have asked, "Where is our home?" and we struggled to answer.

You might even have personal experience with the sad truth that foreigners seldom have rights. When you don't belong, many people treat you differently, and that is not always pleasant. People often blame strangers just because they don't belong.

Yet all these hardships can be a great blessing because these images used by Peter are real and meaningful to the missions heart. We intuitively understand what is meant when Scripture says the world is not our home.

Our experience of "otherness" helps us understand what the Holy Spirit meant when he spoke through Peter and called us to live as "foreigners and exiles." We, better than others in the church, know that as temporary residents in someone else's land, we don't really belong to this world. Therefore, it is normal to be misunderstood at times. It does not surprise us when we sometimes experience the indifference or even hostility of those who are threatened by our unyielding loyalty to another kingdom.

We need to dream of, even cry for, the one place we were meant to experience as home.

Yet as hard as this road can sometimes be, this is exactly the path to which Peter calls all of us. It seems the Holy Spirit wants us to experience enough dislocation stress that we live in a painful longing for our heavenly homeland, a longing so strong, so painful, that we never detour from our calling. This kind of longing can urge us on when we might otherwise give up. We need to dream of, even cry for, the one place we were meant to experience as home. It is the only way we can stay free from the snares of this world. More importantly, this is how we remain true to our King. Living as "foreigners and exiles" means we never allow ourselves to become too comfortable in this world that wars against our souls and our Lord's interests. It reminds us that friendship with the world is enmity with God.

Although this is easier for the missions heart, it will never be easy. It demands that we stiffen our resolve in the middle of a great, lifelong trial. Yet I see the purpose of God in this. Since the missions heart knows what it is to live with the unfulfilled longing of a stranger, we can lead the way for our brothers and sisters. We can demonstrate the meaning of being an alien in this world.

Furthermore, the strange idea that we choose to live this way may help the rest of our spiritual family to understand that they too are called to walk the difficult path of a stranger. Maybe not physically in a foreign country, but truly as pilgrims on their way to their true homeland.

For Whose Honor?

Whoever speaks on their own
does so to gain personal glory,
but he who seeks the glory of the one who sent him
is a man of truth; there is nothing false about him.
—John 7:18

For whose honor are we working? By whose authority are we sent? It seems that to Jesus these were two sides of the same coin.

In many parts of the world today, the message carried by Western missionaries is rejected, not because of "the offense of the cross" but precisely because their message is not exclusively about that cross. All too often, the gospel people hear from us is mixed with Western church traditions, cultural pride, or even our own personal delusions of importance.

While the missionary often does not perceive this, those who receive us do. They quickly recognize to what and whom our words and good deeds point. They see straight through any facade and understand whether our good name and church traditions are truly what is at stake for us. Therefore, these somewhat harsh words are, in truth, merciful to us. Through them, Jesus reveals something foolish pride may have hidden—it is not always the Father's honor that we are working for.

To reverse this sad state of mission affairs, we must first clarify some questions for ourselves. Are our teachings the "teachings of men" like those of the Pharisees? Who are we trying to please, God or the well-intentioned people back home? These questions, and others like them, we must ask and keep asking ourselves until we are sure.

Jesus, in contrast, had a clear mandate from the Father. He lived and spoke exclusively within that mandate. By doing so, he demonstrated a life of radical reorientation. Everything he did and everything he said radiated honor toward someone else—his heavenly Father. Even his enemies could see that he was not building a power base for himself, and this testified to the truth of his message.

If we would truly live as Jesus did, then our words and deeds would be done with only the Father's honor in mind, never our own.

In this passage, our Master makes it clear that when we speak "on our own," we are trying to impress people. We may not do this consciously, but it is there nonetheless, eating away at our souls like a cancer. More often than we care to admit, we secretly hope people will treat us as some sort of dignitary to whom honor is due. This is the antithesis of our Master's way of life.

If we would truly live as Jesus did, then our words and deeds would be done with only the Father's honor in mind, never our own. Then our work, life, or ministry would clearly demonstrate the will of someone else, as this is the very meaning of being sent. When people see this, the natural result will be that all honor will flow to the one who sent us. Such a life makes it easy for people to see that our faith and good deeds are not really our own, only an extension of his nature in us. Thus, it will be ever clear that deserves all the credit, not us.

When our true aim is the honor of the one who sent us, we promote the reputation and renown of our heavenly Father—not our own or that of our church and culture back home.

8 A Drink Offering

For I am already being poured out
like a drink offering, and the time for my departure is near.
—2 Timothy 4:6

Reading Paul's letters provides a clear example of a branch that was truly connected to the vine. This was a man of great passion whose soul was in continuous intimacy with his Master. Everything Paul did was like sweet fruit growing out of this vital bond. What a beautiful portrait it paints, one that we are quick to embrace.

But here, in what is perhaps his last letter, there is a somewhat darker motif that we must wrestle with. Like much of what Paul was inspired to write, the imagery is powerful if we will but understand what he was referring to. Near the end of his life, through careful word choice, Paul conveys another deep message to us, especially to those with a heart for the nations as he had.

Writing one more time to Timothy, the aged apostle refers to his life as having been a "drink offering." These drink offerings were part of the Old Testament sacrificial system; they were offered with freewill sacrifices. They were never *required* of anyone; the drink offering was a freely given act of devotion to God. It was not associated with guilt or obligation of any kind. But since it was freely given, unlike the other sacrifices, it was also completely consumed. Nothing saved, nothing held back—every last bit was poured out as a holy act of worship.

Let that sink in. Everything poured out. Freely, yes, but destroyed completely. Now stop to realize this was the image the Holy Spirit chose to leave with us from the life of a great missionary.

Paul's personal walk with Jesus was the very fragrance of sweet, spiritual fruit. But his twenty-plus years in public ministry was a cruel winepress that crushed this delicate harvest—crushed until it ran blood red. Is this picture harder to embrace than the vine and branches we so love?

Paul's personal walk with Jesus
was the very fragrance of sweet, spiritual fruit.

Paul's gifts, his talents, his very life, were all completely crushed. Year after year, mission after mission, he was pressed more. He was crushed and pressed until everything in him was spilled out, yet the overflow of the press brought new life everywhere he went. His own life had been a freewill offering on the altar of ministry. The whole of his cup was emptied. The opportunity that Paul had been given to preach the gospel to the peoples of Asia Minor cost him everything.

But as with all parables and images, there is a limit to their metaphor. And this one runs out too. For you see, the grapes are helpless in the press. Paul was not. Every day he had to choose to live with this kind of pressure. At any point along the way, he could have backed off. Who would have blamed him? Yet this was a life willingly poured out, an offering of love, not obligation.

And lest we forget, this was not one great heroic act, like stepping into the path of a bullet for a sure and quick martyrdom. Rather, Paul's life was a day-by-day act of devotion. Some of those days were lived out in the public arena, testifying to the grace of God. But many, if not the majority, were crushings lived out in private, painful worship. These were the days he spent nursing back to health after beatings, or months under house arrest. These were the silent tears that stained his face because of sin in churches he had planted. Each of these was part of a life that was slowly and willingly poured out on the altar.

In a day of mega-discount stores and their 50 percent-off sales, we must remember that lasting fruit cannot be bought at reduced prices. The personal cost of bearing a true missions heart is the same today as it was for Paul. We too must be willing to be "poured out like a drink offering."

9 The Quieted Soul

My heart is not proud, LORD,
my eyes are not haughty; I do not concern myself
with great matters or things too wonderful for me.
But I have calmed and quieted myself,
I am like a weaned child with its mother;
like a weaned child I am content.
—Psalm 131:1–2

The missions heart is faced with a great paradox when digesting these words. We who pursue the Great Commission certainly deal in "great matters," even greater than those of running an ancient Eastern kingdom. We are faced with enormous complexities as we plan global strategies, evangelize unreached people groups, and recruit new workers into the harvest. Yet, like King David before us, we must keep these things from distorting our relationship with God. Therefore, it is important that we learn to do what David did: to rest in God's presence.

Notice the qualifier on which the whole passage turns—"a weaned child." This sets up an unspoken contrast that is vital to the imagery—that is, a weaned child as opposed to one who is still nursing. Every time the nursing child lies in his mother's arms, he is unsettled and fussy because he wants something. He is only satisfied by what his mother can *give*.

The weaned child, on the other hand, is different. She can rest; she can enjoy her mother's arms because she is content just being with the one who loves her. The weaned child has grown beyond the stage of seeing her mother only as someone who gives her what she wants. Now she is beginning to simply enjoy her mother's presence. This contentment is what is meant by the words "I have calmed and quieted myself." What a restful picture of one who can face the ambiguities of a difficult world without stress.

But note that God did not do this for the king. David "calmed and quieted" his own soul. He was forced to work out his relationship with God in the real world. As David did this, he learned something we all must. Life is filled with "great matters" and "things too wonderful" for us. There is no way we can handle all these concerns and pressures. So much is truly beyond our control. The only thing we can control is the posture of our soul toward God. Therefore, we absolutely must find a way to calm and quiet our souls.

There must be more to our relationship with him than how he can help us fulfill our mission or vision.

This one thing is more important than all the tasks demanding our attention. How can we ever expect to hear God's heartbeat for the nations if we are forever a fussy newborn? How will we learn to retell his wonderful story of redemption if we can't stop talking long enough to listen to the quiet moving of his Spirit? We will never understand our own small part in his great tapestry if we are always demanding things, even good things, from God like a restless infant.

There should be, of course, a solid place for intercession and petition in our lives, but we must guard against this becoming the main reason we approach God. There must be more to our relationship with him than how he can help us fulfill our mission or vision.

This psalm was David's way of saying that the pleasure of being near God had grown to be enough for him. He was satisfied with nothing more from God than the reality of his presence. We too must learn to be content with God himself, not what he can do, not what he can give.

Sound easy? Just try it. Try resting in the fact that God is at work in your ministry. Try being so content that you actually stop all your striving. I will wager that the moment you do, a cranky, hungry baby will awaken for milk! The truth is, it requires a resolute heart if we are to still and quiet all the fussy demands inside our souls.

Not only that, but this act of faith requires a paradigm shift inside. We must begin to trust God more—our strategies and plans less. We must begin to really believe that there is power inherent in the seed we call the word of God and worry less about the secondary role of us sowing it. Only then will we be at ease like a weaned child with its mother.

10 Acting in Season

Whoever watches the wind will not plant;
whoever looks at the clouds will not reap.
—Ecclesiastes 11:4

A strong spring wind "might" blow away the topsoil, taking precious seed with it. A late summer downpour "could" make the fields muddy and spoil the harvest. Tomorrow there "may be" . . .

Some will say, "Evangelism does little good in the current atmosphere of Muslim fundamentalism." Another might say, "You should wait until the children are older to make the jump to the field. They are such a handful at this age." On and on goes the never-ending list of problems that could arise. There are always *potentially* adverse conditions—especially for the one looking for them. But then again . . .

It "might" be warm and sunny when the seed enters the ground, allowing it to germinate quickly. The rains "will very likely" come at the right time so the fruit will be sweet and full. And "just maybe" the breezes will be light and refreshing to those in the fields at harvest time. The potential of the next day in the field depends as much on our frame of mind as it does on the weather.

The wise farmer knows the full range of these possibilities and, of course, hopes for the best conditions for his travail, although he has no guarantees. Yet notice the somewhat veiled wisdom of the verse. The verbs "plant" and "reap" both occur at God's appointed times. We call them seasons. They are not driven by the day-to-day weather or by fears of such. Rather, they are part of a much bigger picture.

A diligent farmer often labors in the field *despite* the attending circumstances. He sows when it is the *season* for sowing. He enters the field to reap when it is the *time* of harvest. He works, and works hard, because it is the appointed time to do so. Each season will present its own potential challenges of which he must be aware. But the one who would enjoy the pleasures of the harvest is not overly affected by the direction of the wind or the sight of gathering storm clouds in the sky. If he did, it is unlikely that he would ever feed his family.

A diligent farmer often labors in the field despite the attending circumstances.

If we give too much heed to the wind or other signs in the sky, we will never do anything in God's field! Let us learn from the farmer and find a way to remain unmoved by the things we see in the morning and to be steadfast despite our weary feelings at the end of a long day.

But try as we might, this is not something we ever learn once and for all. It is a lifelong task. Satan and his cohort of dark servants constantly try to bog us down in our thinking about all the things that "might" happen. We will be greatly encouraged if only we will grasp the reason for this.

Our enemy knows that the simple act of our entering the field portends badly for his future. When even the weakest of God's servants sets his hand to the plow, it prophesies the coming collapse of the lies and deceit that have held people in darkness and bondage. Satan knows that every faithful witness to God and his word is greater than all the powers of hell; therefore, he will do anything to keep us from acting.

The humble acts of a farmer, obedience in the appointed seasons, and faithfulness to hard work—these are what change the world and break spiritual strongholds. Therefore, the one who does not stop to look at the signs in the skies, but instead responds in obedience at the appointed times, will be the one who reaps a harvest in due season.

Would Paul Vouch for You?

Epaphras, who is one of you and a servant of Christ Jesus, sends greetings. He is always wrestling in prayer for you, that you may stand firm in all the will of God, mature and fully assured. I vouch for him that he is working hard for you and for those at Laodicea and Hierapolis.

—Colossians 4:12–13

Toward the end of this letter intended for several churches, Paul included a few words concerning his high regard for Epaphras, their human donation to Paul's work. Paul had seen the life and work of this brother in the reality of the field. Now he took an opportunity to speak well of him to the church that had sent him. Can you imagine having the apostle Paul vouch for you? Wouldn't that make a nice footnote in the next newsletter!

But we should remember that in his day, Paul was just one of the brothers. By Paul's own admission, he was not counted among the so-called super apostles, the well-known and eloquent preachers on the early church's speaking circuit. It was only in later generations that Christians began to widely see him as special. In other words, this brief passage represents nothing more than one simple missionary expressing heartfelt respect for another with whom he worked.

If this is the case, then we are confronted with a frightening yet most relevant question: What would our colleagues write about us?

We need not worry if contemporary Christian superstars will extol our virtues on their television shows or radio programs. That is quite unlikely to happen anyway. Rather, we should be concerned about the opinion of the humble men and women who serve, pray, and suffer beside us. Would they write a letter to our supporters about our hard work and prayer life? Could they honestly say to our home churches, "I vouch for them. They are working hard for you."

By Paul's own admission,
he was not counted among the so-called super apostles,
the well-known and eloquent preachers
on the early church's speaking circuit.

Usually, we prefer to talk only about "working for the Lord." We don't want anyone to think we are hirelings, exchanging our lives for a paycheck or the approval of people. In one sense, this is right. It is the Lord of the harvest who calls us into his field. For him alone we labor and strive. But viewed in a slightly different light, we *do* work for the people who support our ministries. They are the conduits that God has chosen to convey his blessings to us, and so we have an obligation regarding how we use the kingdom resources they place in our hands. We should, like Epaphras, be "working hard" for them.

However, any real accountability is only theoretical when it concerns world missions. For most people in the church, missionaries represent an awe-inspiring, faraway world. Missionaries live strange international lives and tell incredible stories about distant places. For this reason, many at home develop a surreal picture of who and what they are. Since many in the pews cannot even imagine the missionary's life, they tend to idealize them as if they were a saint on a National Geographic safari. Or a secret agent with a Bible instead of a gun. Consequently, most of our friends in the church cannot possibly be a source of real accountability for us.

That's why we need to seriously think about our witness and work ethic in front of the people who know us as we really are, our colleagues and teammates. Unlike those back home, they are not impressed by a 250-word vocabulary in some new language, especially when, by now, it should be ten times that much! Their opinion is a necessary reality check. In fact, a good reputation among our colleagues is of far greater eternal significance than the accolades of our starstruck friends back home.

Epaphras, whoever this obscure brother was, had just such a high reputation among his coworkers. His life had been such a credit to the kingdom that someone was willing to write a letter commending him to his sending church. All missionaries should aspire to a life like Epaphras, even though the apostle Paul will not be doing the writing.

Our Very Great Reward

Do not be afraid, Abram.
I am your shield, your very great reward.
—Genesis 15:1

Here we see God, the great I Am, offering himself to a man. The one who holds the galaxies in the palm of his hand, who spoke the entire universe into existence, this one above all others was giving himself in a relationship to Abram. God appears to Abram in a vision and calls himself a "very great reward"—yet even that is an understatement!

On this particular day, poor Abram seems to be suffering from desert blindness. If I read this correctly, the old man completely missed the point because immediately following such a profound personal promise, he asked this unsearchable God, "What can you give me since I remain childless?" How could Abram ask for anything else when the one who is life itself was offering his very person to him?

Nevertheless, before we start to feel too superior, we should painfully admit that we often suffer the same affliction. This same God has offered himself to us in the face of Jesus, yet we often reply, "And what will you do for today?" We are given the eternal reward of living in the presence of the God of glory, but we end up asking him to pay the light bill!

Yet in reading this passage, we see that God, who is rich in mercy, did not rebuke Abram for missing the magnitude of his offer. He knew that this simple, shortsighted bedouin would someday understand. I think this God of Abram understands that most of the time the spiritual desert we call the "here and now" seems much more real to us than his offer of eternal reward. He understands the limitations of time and space that make the realm of his kingdom hard for us to grasp.

Try as we might, we often end up like our father Abram—asking for cheap costume jewelry when gold, silver, and precious stones cannot begin to describe the riches being offered.

I believe God knew that Abram could not grasp the profound nature of the offer he was making that day, and like a gracious bridegroom, he was not easily offended. He knew that his beloved could not possibly understand the extent of his love until the wedding, until the day when the fullness of his riches and generosity would be on display for a waiting universe to see.

We try to appreciate his offer to us. We read about it, sing about it, sometimes even meditate on it. But in the end, we are much like Abram, blinded by the struggles of the pilgrim's journey. For the missions heart, the stays at the oasis are short; the crossings of the deserts long. Sometimes our vision is no further than one blinding sandstorm after another. It is especially at times like these that we also ask the great I Am, "What can you give me?"

Yet in the end, the hardships of the desert proved to be the fertile soil Abram's faith needed to grow. It was there that he slowly came to understand the true nature of the one who was calling to him. And even today, to modern spiritual bedouins like us, he offers, "I am your shield, your very great reward." Therefore, no matter what kind of spiritual desert you find yourself in, take heart. Like his love toward Abram before us, despite our nearsightedness, God is pleased to call us deeper into his intimacy.

God is pleased to call us
deeper into his intimacy.

Remember, it was this weak and at times faithless man who was later called the "friend of God."

13 To See Him Who Is Invisible

He persevered because he saw him who is invisible.
—Hebrews 11:27

Could this be one of those glorious moments when Scripture opens its treasure chest and brings out, in plain sight, the answer to a thousand secret prayers? In the middle of a long list that we call the "faith hall of fame," we have this little statement, almost an aside, about Moses. At first, it seems a bit out of context, lacking further explanation. But perhaps none is needed.

In less than ten words, we see how a penniless fugitive was changed into one of the greatest leaders the world has ever known. The answer is both simple and profound. Moses saw God. A striking paradox happened in the life of Moses; he saw the one who cannot be seen. He encountered the one who is wholly other, who is beyond knowing.

People often assume that the writer of Hebrews had the burning bush in mind when he penned these words, and maybe he did. Then again, maybe he didn't. What if he was referring to something deeper than a single event in Moses's life? Could it be that this seeing of God was more of a lifelong journey, growing into the ability to see him who is beyond physical sight? What if it was more like an inner vision carried about in the heart of the great prophet?

Whatever it might have been, this seeing of God was the source of Moses's strength. It was a compass that he could personally return to repeatedly when he needed to regain his bearings.

Moses faced tremendous pressure, first from Pharaoh and then repeatedly from God's dearly beloved and grumbling people. Through the years, he endured much—times of unbearable demand on his leadership and more than a few life-and-death struggles. Yet again and again, he persevered. Somehow, the God whom Moses "saw" had a far greater impact on him than all the fury of an earthly monarch or the desolation of a howling desert wasteland. His vision of the living God was even more real to him than a horde of backbiting, discouraged followers. And over the centuries, what was a personal anchor for Moses has grown to become a powerful example for us.

A striking paradox happened in the life of Moses; he saw the one who cannot be seen.

If only this vision had been easy for Aaron's younger brother to discover—unfortunately, it was not. Even a superficial reading gives the impression of a life filled with difficulty and despair. His personal victories were great, but long were the years between those triumphs. Yet, I believe there was something about these years of hardship that helped cultivate a heart that could see this God who is not seen.

We, on the other hand, have a much better offer. To "see God," we need only look to him who is the "image of the invisible God," Jesus. The living Word has made God manifest since he is the "radiance of God's glory and the exact representation of his being."

We don't have to spend half a lifetime wandering the desert to see our God clearly. We are only required to spend our lives gazing intently into his word. We have been promised that we will find him when we seek him with all our hearts. And when we do, neither the tirades of men on the outside nor fears and doubts on the inside will shake our faith in him whom we have seen. With such a lifelong, all-transforming vision, we may even join the ranks of men like Moses who changed their world.

Washing Feet

Jesus knew that the Father
had put all things under his power,
and that he had come from God and was returning to God;
so he got up from the meal, took off his outer clothing,
and wrapped a towel around his waist . . .
and began to wash his disciples' feet
—John 13:3–5

Once again, Jesus is a marvelous paradox. In the upper room stood the Creator, the one to whom countless angels ever offer ageless worship. Yet because he was so completely sure of this eternal reality, Jesus stepped down to the lowest possible place in the room. Here, the greatest of all shocks us by acting as if he were the least. In doing so, his actions that night were the consummate example of the power that comes from knowing who you are.

Unlike us, Jesus had nothing to prove to anyone in the room. He didn't feel compelled to impress his disciples. He had no ego needing to be stroked by the conversation around the table. He was totally secure in his relationship to the Father; therefore, he was free. He was free to take authority over the temple districts and drive out the merchants in the morning or kneel as a lowly houseboy in the evening. On this night, at the beginning of his passion, Jesus draped himself with a slave's towel and washed dirt, grime, and camel dung from his disciples' feet. Can we even begin to fathom the power of that moment?

But since the disciples had a habit of missing the point, Jesus followed up his living parable with these words recorded in verse 15: "I have set for you an example that you should do as I have done for you." Do we think he was only talking about washing dirty feet?

Oh, if only we would follow this example! If we had the same confidence in our relationship with our heavenly Father, then we would be so much more settled in our callings. Perhaps we could stop doing ministry to impress people. We would no longer need the flattery of a church world that usually flocks after the famous, the important, and those who can "pack the house."

If we had the same confidence in our relationship with our heavenly Father, then we would be so much more settled in our callings.

Such a confidence would empower us to really live out our callings. We would no longer have to look over our shoulders to see who was watching and noticing our good deeds. We would not worry about the reviews. We could tenderly serve the lowly, destitute, and dying. Then, if needed, we would stand up and rebuke the rich and powerful—the ones who usually support us.

Unfortunately, the realm of world missions is not immune to the effects of wealth and affluence; they have drawn us too into the spirit of the age. However, if we were truly secure as our Father's children, many of the structures in the church world would come crashing down because they have been constructed to maintain a facade. So much of what is done in Jesus's name, even on the mission field, is little more than props for position and power, the opposite spirit of the one who wore the towel that night. If the day ever comes when we are as confident in who we are as our Master, that will be a day when the angels sing a new song, and the powers of darkness will tremble.

Jesus's confidence was not tied to position, power, or anything else people could offer—because people were not the source of his ministry. Jesus very simply knew who he was. His personality was thoroughly grounded in his purpose and mission. And this anchor empowered him to serve the disciples and us with the most striking example of humility that the world has ever seen.

Useless Garbage

What is more,
I consider everything a loss because of the surpassing worth
of knowing Christ Jesus my Lord, for whose sake
I have lost all things. I consider them garbage,
that I may gain Christ and be found in him.
—Philippians 3:8–9

Paul's words here are so noble, so profound, and so easy to spiritualize. Could it be that we have forgotten this was real, that Paul actually lived this way? We may have studied the methods of the great apostle, which are indeed a wonderful example to follow, but how hard have we tried to emulate his lifestyle?

For some reason, I've never seen a seminary catalog with any course called "Following Paul's Example of Personal Loss 101." Nor can I remember anything on the shelf of our Christian bookstore entitled *10 Ways to Lose All Things*.

But if we are serious about reaching the nations, we need to understand the impact that Paul's lifestyle had on his ministry, that is, if we really desire the same results. Is it possible that Paul could say and do the things he did *only* because of the way he lived? Missions, we must remember, is much more than methods.

Jesus did not say to the first disciples, "You will go about witnessing." He told them, "You will be my witnesses." Big difference. The Master's intention was that his servants would be living, breathing incarnations of the message he gave them. One of the main reasons for Paul's phenomenal success was that his life itself became a witness to Jesus Christ, a manifestation of the message.

But such identification comes at a cost. The price Paul willingly paid, day in and day out, was that he no longer measured himself by the standards of this world. Our culture asks us, "What things do you own? What is your social status? What valuable things have you accomplished with your life?"

But the man who grew up as a young religious aristocrat from Tarsus could not answer these relatively universal questions, for that man was dead. In fact, Paul so counted his life "hid with Christ in God" that the life and deeds of his Master were the only measure of himself that now mattered.

Make no mistake,
the way we live out our calling
is profoundly important.

Paul was a walking epistle. Everything he said, everything he did, spoke of his Master. This unspoken message was especially eloquent because of how he handled those things that had previously been to his profit. He insisted that everything on which he had once so carefully built his personal significance was now only a pile of rot.

The imagery evokes the filth and stench that can sometimes assault the senses in remote parts of the world. Do I truly regard my status in society as I do the heaps of rotting vegetables that I see out my window each morning? Do I consider my personal achievements to have the same odor as a putrid animal carcass that may occasionally crown the pile?

If we allow it, Paul's words stop being theory and begin to meddle in our lives. Make no mistake, the way we live out our calling is profoundly important. Can I honestly say that the things that formerly made me feel important are now only a loss? Are my personal achievements and status now garbage to me?

Paul held everything about himself with contempt whenever it crossed paths with his knowing Christ. He was able to walk so freely detached from the world because he now saw himself only in relation to his redeemer. Everything that had previously defined him in this world was now but a stench to his nostrils. When we live this same way, it shapes people's perception of the message we bring. These two—the message we speak and the message of our lifestyle—are much more intertwined than most of us care to admit.

My Redeemer Lives

I know that my redeemer lives. . . .
And after my skin has been destroyed,
yet in my flesh I will see God; I myself will see him
with my own eyes—I, and not another.
How my heart yearns within me!
—Job 19:25–27

Was this the lament of a man at the end of his rope, or the cry from a heart sold out to eternity?

Job was certainly living through a test far worse than any of us have known. So it could be that we are simply hearing the words of complete despair, of one who was in so much pain he wished ed for death to come. Honestly, it would be understandable if his words were bitteranguish seeping out of his soul.

But deep inside, I secretly hope we are seeing something else here from Job. I want to believe, and in fact do, that this verse is the cry of a man who was yearning for eternity. Not because of the hardships of this life but despite them.

Job yearned to see this redeemer of his, and somehow, he knew he would. Long before anyone would know his name as Jesus, Job affirmed that the greatest thing that could ever happen to someone was to see the one who would call himself "the resurrection and the life."

Of course, we really don't know how or when Job came to this deep insight, but that is of no importance. For whether it comes through pain, divine revelation, or the witness of another, the only thing that matters is that we acquire such a deep yearning for Christ that in life or death, he alone is our greatest desire!

Through most of Job's narrative, we see him struggling to comprehend the pain through which he was living. But here, embedded in the middle of his personal story, we are given a short declaration of a faith that is later revealed to be pleasing to God. For that reason, it is most important. A faith that can stand through the kinds of fires that Job endured is a faith worth imitating.

Job yearned to see this redeemer of his, and somehow, he knew he would.

In these brief few words, Job affirmed from where his salvation would come. He showed that the answer is not derived from understanding life or its afflictions. That he had tried, but to no avail. Rather, his hope for this life and the next would only be found in the face of the one he would someday see. This is a profound truth, mined from intense pain. Do we really want God alone, or do we want his blessings?

To behold Job's God, even for a moment, would far surpass everything else he had ever known. The riches he had amassed and the sorrow he had bitterly drunk would all be lost in the glory of one moment of seeing this Redeemer God.

What a vision! What a statement of faith! Despite everything his five senses were screaming at him, Job earnestly believed that death was only a passageway to the moment he longed for. He feared not the rot of the grave because he knew its weakness could never overcome the strength of the great Redeemer who would someday come for him.

When Job's world had fallen apart, and his own strength seemed to be ebbing away, he still knew his hope was alive and well. Even when he could not understand the "why" of it all, he would trust in the one who he would someday see with his very own eyes. This yearning was the source of Job's hope and is ours as well.

Thankfully, the life of the missions heart is not always as harsh as those bitter days for Job. Still, life without a vision of our future redemption is a life with little to look forward to. As those who live with an eye to the future, the missions heart must share Job's hope, even if we have thankfully not shared the depth of his pain. Yes, we too know our Redeemer lives and must daily choose to live with that eternal longing.

Well Done!

His master replied,
"Well done, good and faithful servant!
You have been faithful with a few things;
I will put you in charge of many things.
Come and share your master's happiness!"
—Matthew 25:23

These words should be deeply engraved into every missions heart, indeed, into every heart that has ever received a gift from the Master. They stand like a great monolith at the trailhead, calling us forward, reminding us of what is ahead.

The promise found in this parable is so grand that we can scarcely comprehend it this side of heaven. The thought of hearing the Lord of lords commend us in this way is almost too much for the human mind to grasp. For this reason, I am afraid we spend far too little time meditating on it. Therefore, let us now try to enter this spectacular moment, if only for a fleeting glimpse.

The beauty of a thousand rainbows fills the limitless sky as we stand on a sparkling sea of crystal. We are surrounded by a vast army of angels who are now standing silent; endless worship is quieted just for this moment. Then, in steps the King of kings, the one to whom they have always sung their eternal song.

The heavenly hush grows profound as the Master takes time to call in his servants, one by one. And then, before the eyes of all heaven, this unbelievably great one calls you. The Master whom you have served through a lifetime, the face you have longed for through many trials, speaks your name. Trembling seizes you like a woman in the final moments of labor.

Whether your gifts were great or small, whether your name was known or lost in the avalanche of history, now your life is revealed for what it truly was—an offering of faithful love to the one who commissioned you. Then, before the countless heavenly host, the King commends your little part in the cosmic drama that has just ended. He knows that all the good things you did were but expressions of his valiant heart, yet he still stoops to reveal some of his glory in you.

Whether your gifts were great or small, whether your name was known or lost in the avalanche of history, now your life is revealed for what it truly was—an offering of faithful love to the one who commissioned you.

The King, merciful as he is, does not at this moment remind you of the many times you could have done more, nor does he rehearse your sins so the angels can shame you. Instead, he commends you. He commends you simply for the fact that you were faithful to his call. Standing before him in eternity, nothing else matters, and nothing else is said.

There are so many ways we have all failed the Master, so many things we have lived to regret, but those do not belong to this moment. This great and fearful day is only for words of approval to those who have welcomed his purpose in their lives. Can we even imagine it?

Whatever pain we suffered in order to release the fragrance of his love in dark places is now forgotten. The trials and difficulties that plagued our path now seem so insignificant in the light of his face. For years you tried to believe that this day would really come, but at times it was so hard. The idea of his smile seemed so far away in comparison to the struggles of this life or the contempt of the world, which was often at hand.

And now, as heaven and earth stand still to hear his words of loving approval to you, somewhere in the back of your mind you remember words from our brother Paul: "For our light and momentary troubles are achieving for us an eternal glory that far outweighs them all." And you think—"Yes, Paul. You were right!"

A Great Cloud of Witnesses

Therefore, since we are surrounded by such a great cloud of witnesses, let us throw off everything that hinders and the sin that so easily entangles. And let us run with perseverance the race marked out for us.
—Hebrews 12:1

The writer of Hebrews points the persecuted Jewish Christians back toward those who so faithfully lived a life of faith in the past. This great "faith hall of fame," as we sometimes call Hebrews 11, was written to be an encouragement for them to press on.

The missions heart, likewise, has a great cloud of witnesses to urge us on as we struggle to complete the Great Commission. The seats in this missions hall of fame are filled with champions like Hudson Taylor, Adoniram Judson, and Lottie Moon. Their vision, perseverance, and sacrifice call out to us as a reminder of the price that must be paid for the heartbeat of God to be known in new lands and cultures.

These men and women gave completely of themselves. They lived, and often died, with little reward in this life. Their only thought was the good pleasure of their Master; the spread of his great name and renown was their only purpose.

Only posterity recognized their nobility; to their own generation, they were often an enigma. Yet, we now look back on their examples as testimony to the power of God to work miracles whenever he finds a willing heart through whom he can speak. This is the great cloud of witnesses who urge us on.

And what more can we say? As the writer of Hebrews put it, time does not allow us to tell of the multitude of others, a nameless army, who fill the missions history written only in heaven. The call of "Whom shall I send? And who will go for us?" was heard by these hearts, and like Isaiah, they responded—"Here I am. Send me."

For most, our testimony will be unknown to the crowds, written only on the hearts of new sons and daughters for the King.

These unknown servants of God—unknown on earth only—changed their world through simple obedience to their call. Some lived poured-out lives as pilgrims in foreign lands, where they preached the good news to the poor, proclaimed freedom to the captives, and brought sight to the blind.

Others spent a lifetime as living sacrifices on the home front, praying and giving, rejoicing and grieving, so that the work of the kingdom would go forward. Like their brothers and sisters on the front lines, these missions hearts faced battles unknown to most of the church. They spent years on their knees, slowly intertwining their hearts to peoples and places that their eyes would never see. While unnoticed on the earth, their tears were recorded, one by one, as the seed for harvests they could only receive by faith.

Yet the fruit of their unseen labors are transformed tribes, converted continents, and mass movements to Christ through history. Their names may never again be spoken on earth, but their reward will be great on the day the King rewards his own before angels and men.

It is to such a great cloud that we are called to add our witness. Someone reading this little book may be a Hudson Taylor or Lottie Moon in this generation. But for most, our testimony will be unknown to the crowds, written only on the hearts of new sons and daughters for the King. Let us take courage and not lose heart. The day will come when together with these voices of the past, we will receive the reward that we have so longed for.

Bearing Fruit

Remain in me, as I also remain in you.
No branch can bear fruit by itself; it must remain in the vine.
Neither can you bear fruit unless you remain in me. . . .
Apart from me you can do nothing.
—John 15:4–5

As much as we like to claim to believe the Bible, we often act as though we do not. If these words of Jesus were twisted to reflect the way we normally live, they would read something more like this—"intimate fellowship with me will produce *better* fruit." Or perhaps, "Your fruit will be somewhat less when you drift away from me."

But that is not what our Master said. With the sound of a sharp chisel on stone, his words cut into our hearts. Apart from him, we will produce nothing. Zero. Zilch. Absolutely nothing of eternal value. Are those words hard to receive? Do they feel like a slap in the face to our well-honed religious sensibilities? Deep inside, I think that's exactly how Jesus intended his words to be taken.

For in spite of the religious veneer, most of us don't live like we believe this truth. We act as if we can get by, even do well, thank you, when we are living estranged from the vine. Our committee meetings, urgent emails, and the endless demands of the modern era have become the reality from which we derive our life rather than from an organic union with the one who spoke in the upper room that night.

It's not that we would ever consciously distance ourselves from Jesus; in our heart of hearts, we really do desire intimacy. But when the cold of separation creeps into our relationship with him, it is the rare disciple indeed who immediately stops to lament, "I am undone! My ministry is now pointless, for he is not the very air I breathe."

As sure as the changing of seasons, what we subconsciously believe eventually becomes the way we live. If we believe, even for a moment, that we can produce anything of eternal value apart from the true vine, we soon find ourselves doing just that. We become so busy doing "wonderful things for Jesus" that our inner man is no longer transformed by the wonder of his words. In this state, we find ourselves working ever harder for something that is impossible to achieve—human effort yielding spiritual fruit.

But as disciples who claim to believe the Master's words, we must tremble at the thought of living apart from our life's source in the vine.

It seems to me the main problem is that we generally allow far too high an opinion of our self-driven diligence. We are not convinced that even our most saintly efforts are only shriveled, dead wood trying to bear sweet, juicy fruit. But as disciples who claim to believe the Master's words, we must tremble at the thought of living apart from our life's source in the vine.

Therefore, we must have a healthy fear of the hectic compulsion that saturates our modern world, a pattern that leads only to running our race in fruitless vanity. This would help us feel an urgency whenever the vital, intimate connection to the vine is even nicked by the busyness that plagues our age. Then, we might finally stop our striving good deeds and place our relationship with Jesus on a plane far above our serving of him.

Those of us who are seeking to extend his kingdom must meditate on these profound words of Jesus. Indeed, they must take deep root in the missions heart: "Apart from me you can do nothing." Although spoken on a Judean hillside two thousand years ago, they are just as relevant now, perhaps even more so. If we are not completely convinced of this truth, we will become living parables of the very vanity that Jesus warned against.

Who Is Sending You?

The LORD turned to him [Gideon] and said,
"Go in the strength you have. . . .
Am I not sending you?"
—Judges 6:14

We all know the story of Gideon, the so-called mighty warrior, although we sometimes forget that he was a man who needed multiple miraculous signs while he was hiding in a winepress. Such was the expression of his faith or, more properly, his lack thereof.

Many truths, countless sermons, and probably a few myths have been drawn from this encounter between a frightened man and the living God, but there is one true point we must not miss. It is found in this rhetorical question from the Lord to this great man of doubt. I can almost hear a "voice of many waters" asking—"Am I not sending you?"

Now, we should stop for a moment to ask, "Is there anything else that really matters in world mission?"

What does it matter if the enemies are great or small? Of what consequence are the dangers of the task? If we are sure that the one who calls forth the dawn is the same one who compels us to go, what else do we need to know?

Yes, in the realm of theory, I do at times take this stand. After all, sitting behind my desk with pen and paper makes this easy to confess such great faith. But the moment I step out into the real world, I am quickly reminded that I am but lowly dust—far less the "mighty man of faith" than I aspire to be. Therefore, we should deal honestly with this text and, by extension, with the realities of our human nature.

Let us briefly review Gideon's situation. He was facing real, physical enemies. His hiding was caused by a tangible and present fear. There were cunning men with battle-hardened blades who roamed the countryside in search of loot and blood. His own people were disorganized and leaderless, easy prey in a time of great peril. Gideon knew these things all too well.

For the missions heart,
there is only one question to be asked—
Who is sending me?

With this backdrop as a reality check, we can understand why our hero needed someone much greater than his father and other backers in the clan if he were to fulfill his destiny. He even needed someone of greater weight than the assembled armies of Israel—and so do we.

It is important for missionaries to have the support of loving friends at home in our churches; for these we should thank God. It is most helpful to be sent by godly organizations and their systems. And it is encouraging to be surrounded by valiant co-laborers who support us in the task. But these simply are not enough.

Even the best-intentioned, most spiritually minded people cannot carry the load that "sending" implies—for the sending of missionaries into a complex world of terrorism, technology, and spiritual hunger is an enormous responsibility. It requires a reach completely beyond the greatest human ability. It demands a depth of wisdom that even Solomon would covet. No, we need one who is much greater.

We need a friend who is not hindered by time or distance. We need a sender whose resources are not affected by budget cuts or economic downturns. We need one whose reach goes even beyond the vale of death to offer life eternal to those called to offer the ultimate witness.

For these reasons and more, God's rhetorical question to a frightened Gideon lies at the core of the issue for the missions heart. We cannot consider the obstacles we will face. Nor can we be overly concerned about the resources with which we are to attempt great things. No, for the missions heart, there is only one question to be asked—Who is sending me?

And if, like Gideon before us, the answer returns to us as a blaze of holy fire, let us rise up in what little strength we have and do whatever we are called to do. Being sent by him is truly enough.

His Yoke

Come to me, all you who are weary and burdened,
and I will give you rest. Take my yoke upon you
and learn from me, for I am gentle and humble in heart,
and you will find rest for your souls.
For my yoke is easy and my burden is light.
—Matthew 11:28–30

Weariness. Exhaustion. Complete fatigue. Do any of these sound familiar? For those with a missions heart, these are sometimes close companions. Far too often, a burden *for* the world becomes the burden *of* the world. What began with joy grows into a personal, unrelenting drain on the heart and mind. Is this the way it is supposed to be? Is looking at a world map or out the window *supposed* to cause such a deep, painful sigh?

When we read this passage, physical and spiritual exhaustion does not seem to be what Jesus was offering his disciples as they walked together on the warm Judean hillsides. In fact, if we take Jesus at his word, it is just the opposite, for he said that walking with him would be an easy yoke and light burden. What then has gone wrong? Why is it that so many with a missions heart feel so overburdened and weary as they pursue the calling on their lives?

Perhaps the key is found in Jesus's use of a little yet most instructive word, *my*. *My* yoke, *my* burden, he tells us. We must be forever vigilant that we do not load down our hearts with anything other than the burden that Jesus himself has given us. For you see, there are many honorable and spiritual-sounding weights that can encumber the soul.

For example, there is a great difference between compassion for the poor and feeling the need to fix their poverty. Remember, it was Jesus who said, "The poor you will always have with you." Or likewise, a passion for the salvation of souls is not the same as trying to save them ourselves. There is only one mediator between God and man, and you can rest assured it is not you!

While we know this, it is often in a head knowledge sort of way, which means the lines can become blurred in the heat of battle. It is easy to unconsciously load ourselves with the extra weight of responsibilities that were never ours to bear. Thus, the missions heart can become burdened and weary, not because they are disciples of Jesus, but rather because they have moved away from that position.

Sometimes the best thing the busy and exhausted missions heart can do is to stop.

Our first step back toward a right position is to remember that wearing only the yoke that Jesus gives will bring rest to our souls. This is evidenced by peaceable fruit in our lives and families. By contrast, burdens we take upon ourselves often beat down our spiritual life and leave scars on the ones closest to us. In fact, the end results of such self-initiated good works usually demonstrate that they never were a gift from our kind Master.

Sometimes the best thing the busy and exhausted missions heart can do is to stop. Stop working. Stop serving. Stop trying to do it all. Then, use this deliberate break in schedule to spend time in prayer and personal reflection. A few simple questions often clear the hubris: What, exactly, are the things Jesus gave me to do? And conversely, What have I been loaded down with by myself or others?

We must cultivate a lifelong habit of distinguishing God-given dreams from the many other good things that can weigh down our hearts. Regaining clarity of purpose and vision will often stem the tide of spiritual exhaustion and bring us back to the feet of our gentle and humble Master. A cultivated practice of living more reflectively is a great preventive for spiritual burnout, and more effective than a holiday or retreat *after* hitting the wall. While nothing is wrong with a refreshing trip to the seashore or a visit to a mountain cabin, God is most clearly found in simple obedience to the call on our lives.

22 Contentment as a Spiritual Discipline

I know what it is to be in need,
and I know what it is to have plenty. I have learned the secret
of being content in any and every situation.
—Philippians 4:12

Paul's words here seem to drift out of a dream world. It can be most difficult to connect with them because of something woven deeply into our modern culture—consumerism. In magazines, on the internet, and even in the church, we feel a constant tug toward a happiness that is based on owning the newest book, look, or electronic gadget. In pop culture this relentless drag produces a riptide of self-indulgent sin, dragging us into the depths of despair while advertisers claim their latest product will satisfy our souls.

Many Christians are so constantly assaulted by consumerism that they have become oblivious to it, unable to see the corrosive effects of this culturally acceptable form of greed. Of course, this is a bit harder for those of us who live among the world's poor and destitute, but even the softest heart can grow calluses from living in denial.

When exposed for what it is, it is easy to see that this is not God's purpose for his servants. He did not enable us to see a lost and hurting world only for us to later become blinded by what James calls the "lust of the eyes."

But what can we do? How do we live out our calling when this undertow pulls for control of every decision we make?

To begin with, the missions heart should recognize that we are not alone in this struggle. The apostle Paul was a man who had been groomed in the corridors of Judaism's power at Jerusalem. He likely had access to more than average wealth in his first-century world. In a relative way, it would be accurate to say that the economic descent he made to fulfill his calling was similar to what many missions hearts must make today when they leave the developed world.

Very simply, he had learned what it means to be content.

But somewhere along this downward leading path, Paul learned what he later called his "secret." Everyone loves to hear a secret. It makes us an insider and puts us in touch with those in the know. And so it is with this secret the Holy Spirit taught the apostle Paul. I say taught by the Holy Spirit because this secret did not come naturally to Paul, nor will it for any of us. Yet, if we can grasp what he was saying here, we will move into a completely new quality of life with God. So, just what was the great secret of the aged apostle?

Very simply, he had learned what it means to be *content.*

He had learned to be satisfied with whatever the Lord provided him, at ease, even when his living situation was less than comfortable. There is nothing terribly complicated about the basic idea, but the ramifications of living it out are enormous. What would happen if we started being truly happy with what we have? What if we stopped wanting more, no matter what is being offered to us in the marketplace? Our clothes, cars, and computers would plummet in value to us, and the relative value of the people around us would surge. In short, such contentment would revolutionize our lives and ministries—and perhaps put a few retailers out of business.

But such a massive shift of worldview will not come easy, not even for the missions heart. Considering the state of modern society, I would say that entering a true state of contentment will require such focus and zeal that it could properly be described as a "new" spiritual discipline—specifically, the discipline of simplicity.

But if we would diligently practice this posture of the soul long enough for it to become habitual, then we would learn, as did Paul, that God himself is truly all we need. His presence in our lives can free us from the soulish anxiety that arises from our unmet desires. In a consumer-saturated twenty-first century, Paul's simple words stand out as a safe harbor that protects the soul from the storm of materialistic anxiety—something even the missions heart needs from time to time.

A Strong Tower

The name of the LORD is a fortified tower;
the righteous run to it and are safe.
—Proverbs 18:10

The beautiful picture painted by Solomon's words was a common sight in his day—one that would clearly speak to those for whom it was first intended. But much has changed in the past three thousand years, so it would do us good to try to grasp the historical context of these words.

Try to imagine a group of simple peasants working their fields in the midday sun. Their labor is hard, but they enjoy the secure feeling of living among their own people, working their own land for their own benefit. Then, out of nowhere arises a menacing dust cloud. The air slowly fills with the sounds of camels, donkeys, and horses ridden by a band of heavily armed men. The farmers are all but defenseless with nothing but wooden hoes. Furthermore, the speed of the ominous strangers' advance leaves them no time to run to their homes in the village. Working out in the open fields, they are dangerously exposed.

Exposed, that is, unless they turn to a place of refuge and safety, a strong rock tower standing nearby on the plain that had been built by their ancestors for just such moments. Its ancient stones could tell stories of bandits and battles, of sandstorms and blinding blizzards. Yet, it has outlasted them all, a mute testimony to its great strength in the moment of distress.

Now, the Holy Spirit breathes on this image that was well known to the ancient Israelites and paints an enduring picture for us all. "The name of the LORD is a fortified tower." The Lord's character is a place of refuge, a stronghold in which to hide. To know his ways, his worthy reputation as one who can be trusted, is to have a place to hide in the moment of danger or fear. In him, we have a place to turn. We are not left exposed and at the mercy of any enemy that has come to do us harm. But notice, it is not enough to simply know his name. Many claim to know him, yet it has little effect when they face life's trials. Solomon goes on to say, "The righteous run to it and are safe."

We must toss aside our grown-up pretenses and run like the frightened children we really are when danger approaches.

King David's wise son shows us that the key is found, like in many other areas in life, in the verbs. He says that we must "run" to the Lord. We must toss aside our grown-up pretenses and run like the frightened children we really are when danger approaches. We must forget our pride and run, not walk, to him.

Amid the difficulties and dangers of this life, there is no place for bravado and the distorted version of courage it represents. We must not be ashamed to unmask our facade of worldly dignity and admit there is only one whose strength can save us. Our wealth is of no value in the day of trouble, and we cannot enlighten our enemies with our education. The things in which we often place our trust will do us no good in this moment. We have one hope. We must flee to the tower of strength who waits for us, arms outstretched to receive his children.

When we do, his name proves to be a fortification standing amid the brutalities of life. Come what may, he has weathered it before. Like footsteps on a stone stairway, the voices of those who trusted him in the past echo their testimony for us if we will but listen. We can trust that he will eternally enfold us in his strength and that he always waits to hide us in his love, but only for those who are humble enough to run to him.

Wellspring of Life

Above all else, guard your heart,
for everything you do flows from it.
—Proverbs 4:23

The heart is where the action is.

It is the wellspring, the living fountain, the source of what we say and who we are. Contrary to the ethos of this age, it is not the outer man—our newsletters, websites, or Instagram pages—that run the show. It is the deep, heart-level motivations that determine the direction our life flows.

This is a crucial issue for the missions heart, and even that is putting it lightly, because we are first and foremost defined by our hearts. We are not distinguished by our professions or educational profiles, for they are varied. Not even the location we live can describe us, for a calling to the nations may very well mean staying at home, wherever that may be. Rather, Great Commission Christians comprise a loose federation, a group of people whose unity is found in a mutual passion and the desire for the glory of God to be revealed to all nations. We are characterized by our hearts.

This calling to the nations is no more than the overflowing of a heart that is full, a heart so full of desire that it seeks outlet. If you are truly running this race we call world missions, the reason is simple—nothing else would satisfy the longing of your soul. And if you are to stay on track for the long haul, each new day's sacrifice must flow from a heart sold out to the King.

So important is this principle of living from our hearts that all diligence is required, or we quickly degenerate into a union of religious professionals punching a clock for some great bureaucracy in the sky. If we allow ourselves to lapse into apathy, fear, or cold professionalism, we taint the stream of blended human-divine passion. We did not create this flow, but ours is the task of safeguarding the small portion of the stream that flows through us.

Guarding our hearts really is that important, because this heart of ours is all we actually have to offer.

That is why our hearts deserve the highest security. We must place strong sentries at the gate and inspect all who try to gain entrance. Like well-trained guards at a dangerous international border, we must carefully inspect the baggage of each and every visitor, for those things that cross into our territory will soon take up residence and become a part of who we are.

In this day of advertising extremes and overstatement, "guarding the heart" is an understatement. We should instead shout—Call up the National Guard! Guarding our hearts really is that important, because this heart of ours is all we actually have to offer. Therefore, to the missions heart, this snippet of wisdom from King David to his young son becomes even more urgent. The reality of living out our hearts puts us in a position that is to be both pitied and greatly envied. We absolutely must guard our hearts with all the zeal we can muster.

However, the truth is that we do live from our hearts, whatever that may be. We can live with passion and purpose, allowing that to be the flow from which those downstream imbibe. Or we can be careless and allow the source to become polluted and putrid. But either way, out of our hearts will flow the direction of our lives and thus what we offer to the nations.

There are no options. The heart is where the action is. Always and forever.

Harassed and Helpless

Jesus went through all the towns and villages,
teaching in their synagogues, proclaiming the good news
of the kingdom and healing every disease and sickness.
When he saw the crowds, he had compassion on them,
because they were harassed and helpless,
like sheep without a shepherd.
—Matthew 9:35–36

I wonder sometimes if we read this passage too fast. It might be worth slowing down because I believe a key to understanding God's heart toward the lost is found in these verses. More specifically in the wordplay "sheep without a shepherd." The reason I say this is a play on words is that there is really no such thing as sheep without a shepherd, at least for very long. Sheep simply cannot survive as the masters of their own fate.

Sheep need a shepherd like you and I need air. They are completely undone without constant care and supervision. But that is not all. While sheep cannot live for long without a shepherd, conversely, a shepherd without sheep is as meaningless as a fisherman without water. The life of a shepherd is defined by the need others have of him.

As Jesus engaged the world around him, his incarnation was given meaning because he came to care for his sheep. His purpose and his person were intertwined.

Yet as he walked the Judean hillsides, what he saw must have sickened this shepherd's heart. There on open display was all the pain a broken world could dish out. There, he dealt with sickness, disease, and the demonized.

The religious leaders of the day were not being shepherds; therefore, the flock was being taken advantage of in the worst of ways. These helpless sheep were being exposed to the evil schemes of an enemy whom Jesus had known since the rebellion in heaven. In modern vernacular, we might say that the people referred to in this verse were like "children without a parent." Therefore, they were endangered, exposed, and exploited.

Therefore, if we are to understand Jesus's heart for the lost, we must see them as he did—sheep without a shepherd.

In the eyes of Jesus, these were not the dirty, needy crowds that you and I might have seen with our eyes. They were sheep; more than that, they were his sheep. He knew that the pain in their eyes should not be there. They had a better birthright but did not know what it was. Bitterness was so normal that they thought life was meant to be this way, but the great shepherd knew better.

No, he saw into the spiritual backdrop of their lives and recognized the hateful enemy that was using and abusing them as a way to get at their Creator. And Jesus was willing to use his strength to defend them, even to the death.

This was because, at the core of his being, he was a shepherd. I have no doubt that he knew it would be some of these same people who would later cry "crucify, crucify." But that did not, and could not, change matters because it did not change who he was at heart, the great shepherd of the sheep.

Therefore, if we are to understand Jesus's heart for the lost, we must see them as he did—sheep without a shepherd. They are not the thieves who take advantage of us in foreign bazaars, nor are they the mean-spirited officials who sometimes threaten us. They are simply sheep who do not know their shepherd. And just as was the case with Jesus, they are the reason we are sent.

His Lamp Will Keep Burning

You, LORD, keep my lamp burning;
my God turns my darkness into light.
—Psalm 18:28

David wrote this psalm as he reflected on a bitterly difficult time in his life. The psalm reflects on the ten years King Saul had hunted David like a dog. It is not hard to imagine these as years of doubt for David—even perhaps growing into disbelief—that God would ever fulfill his promises. Dark moments had become the norm for so long that all hope in the promises of God was likely a forgotten memory. My guess is that decade was, for David, as close as one might come to "hell on earth."

In your passion for the nations, have you ever been so low that you could feel empathy for the haggard figure of David running from Saul? Have you ever felt that the fire God gave you for missions would never come to fruition, that the promises of God would not turn out true in your life?

If so, then take courage from David's reflection in his later years about that time of pain and disappointment.

Saul's envy had stolen more than just ten years of David's life—it had taken parts of his soul too. The unending disillusionment had crushed to death almost anything that could be called "David." Had you looked beneath the blood and mud-stained face, you just might have seen something of great value.

Saul's crushing hate had taken much from David: his home, his family, maybe even his dignity. But there remained something in him that was eternal—and it was the only thing that survived. This was what David called his "lamp," the thing that burned on through his years of agony.

Today we use different words to describe this eternal spark. Some might speak of David's "destiny." Others would write about his "calling." The words have changed, but the underlying truth remains the same. Somewhere in our heart of hearts there must be a tiny part of God's own great person. This is the "lamp" that David said had burned throughout his dark night of the soul.

Some spend what seems like ages hidden in God's school of preparation before they take their place in the drama of reaching the nations.

The missions heart usually has its own dark night to later reflect on as did David. Some spend what seems like ages hidden in God's school of preparation before they take their place in the drama of reaching the nations. Others give many years, even a lifetime, to their calling with little outward fruit. Some are still today praying, working, yearning for something concrete to show a skeptical world that the passion of their heart really is from God.

Such misery is not the kind of thing that we often talk about, but the simple truth is that the fire of God's presence often burns slow. It may require years, even decades, to burn up all the dross that needs to be consumed in our hearts. It takes time to learn to depend on his passion, not ours, as the inconsumable fuel for the vision he has given us.

For many of us, it takes a long time to realize that the nations will be reached, not because I so greatly desire it but because God himself *so much more greatly* desires it. The passion must be *his*, not *mine*. I am only a steward of this fire, one that was given to me directly from the altar that stands before the throne of God.

While going through the suffering of waiting, the whole affair seems a pointless waste of a unique life and gifts. But it is only through such dark and difficult times that our calling, our lamp, if you will, becomes known for what it is—a God-given destiny. And this is a good thing, for even a warrior like David had to learn that his own iron-hard will could never supply the spiritual oil needed to keep his lamp burning.

Just as David did before us, we must learn that God will sustain the fire that is his own. David looked back and saw that his lamp remained for one reason only: God himself had a personal interest in it being so. Unfortunately, it seems that the vantage point needed to see this valuable lesson comes only through hindsight, and this is a lesson that is never learned in a hurry.

Your Deeds, His Glory

Let your light shine before others
that they may see your good deeds and glorify
your Father in heaven.
—Matthew 5:16

The Christian missions community is known around the world for its mercy and benevolence. Doctors leave lucrative Western practices to tramp across tired, dirty clinic floors and give out the most basic of healthcare. Teachers give up comfort and family to teach in broken, underfunded schools. Engineers leave state-of-the-art design rooms to sketch irrigation plans in the dust of drought-stricken plains.

Why do so many of God's people move to the places that many bright young people are trying hard to leave? Why do they give away their hard-earned professional skills, expecting nothing in return? In other words, why do we do what we do?

On one level, there are as many reasons as there are people. Each is drawn through differing circumstances, with differing goals in life. The means of calling someone to a life in world missions can be as diverse as the shades of green in a rainforest. But on an altogether different level, there is only one reason that God's people should offer themselves and their skills—for his glory.

This is an incredibly important point, for it is the continental divide that separates the missions heart from all the other kind and benevolent types in the world. Countless people want to see starving children fed. Many wish to bring their version of civilization and progress to "backward and underdeveloped" peoples. But philanthropists of this stripe see their help as an end in itself. Not so the missions heart. We understand that our acts of kindness are nothing more than evidence of someone much greater at work.

We want men to see our good deeds and praise our Father in heaven.

However, there is great pressure on the missions heart these days—pressure to conform to a more humanitarian version of world outreach. Many tell us that our work should be nothing more than the compassionate human response to another human's need—leave God out of it, thank you—and everything will be fine. The secular world welcomes our presence as long as we work in this spirit, and we are accepted as colleagues and peers.

At first, this sounds tolerable, a small cost for détente with our colleagues. But with deeper inquiry, we uncover that the humanitarian approach to helping others brings a subtle hook—the funneling of praise and honor to the humanitarians. While this may please the world, it is not why we left home and hearth.

The missions heart must revolt at the idea that our good deeds should bring praise to human kindness.

We know that in our flesh dwells no good thing! We know ourselves well enough to say, with great conviction, that it is neither an inherent goodness of character that carries us to foreign lands nor a magnanimous heart that causes us to stay.

We do these things for one reason only: We want men to see our good deeds and praise our Father in heaven. His glory is the driving force behind all we do. Yet, it is this point that the humanists attack, and so we must be clear. We must weave a concern for the Lord's fame into all our professional work and season our conversations with it as salt. Otherwise, the world may pay tribute to the "kind and benevolent foreigners," but our Father will receive little praise.

Satan will gladly heap glory on our human compassion and cause even our enemies to shower us with praise—anything to keep this little secret in a box. But the missions heart cannot allow this to happen. We have the unrivaled privilege of pointing to the one who sent us, to clearly say to a world of lost sinners that every good and noble thing they see in us is only an expression of a loving heavenly Father who is calling them by name.

28 A Great Multitude Before the Throne

Before me was a great multitude that no one could count,
from every nation, tribe, people and language,
standing before the throne and before the Lamb.
They were wearing white robes and were holding palm branches
in their hands. And they cried out in a loud voice:
"Salvation belongs to our God, who sits on the throne,
and to the Lamb."
—Revelation 7:9–10

Don't read on, just stop and listen. Soak your spirit in the unearthly harmonies of universal worship. This eternal moment is the climax of everything you have dreamed about. This is what countless missions hearts have lived and died for. So stop and listen until it ministers to your soul.

We may not see it in our short day under the sun, but in the life that is to come, we will hear *every* nation worship the only one who is worthy. Someday, you and I will listen to the sound of our hearts' burden bearing eternal fruit.

It sounds good, does it not?

The problem is, sometimes it sounds almost *too* good. If we are honest, it is not always easy to receive these words as the great truth they are. There are times when it sounds too much like a fairy tale. Sometimes, laboring in the Master's harvest field produces calluses on the heart as well as the hands.

Thus, it will do us a great deal of good to stop and listen, every now and again, to the sounds of heaven. To allow, just for a moment, our inner ear to transport us to that great day when *every* nation, *every* tribe, *every* people, and *every* language are represented around the throne.

Listen to the people on your heart as they call to him as "our God." Perhaps you have been stung by harsh words rejecting him as some kind of "foreign god." But now, in the eternal day, such fleeting moments are only a forgotten memory, for now they have tasted of his great salvation and know him for who he really is.

We may not see it in our short day under the sun, but in the life that is to come, we will hear every nation worship the only one who is worthy.

Stop long enough to hear them as they cry out to the Lamb. Can you believe what you are hearing? How many times was your face stained with tears because of their crying out to someone else? Now, they too are washed in that precious blood! Listen as they shout about his great sacrifice.

But don't leave just yet. Allow yourself to linger in the vision a moment longer. There is still one more thing that the missions heart desperately needs to cling to—one more sound that we should hear.

Can you hear it? Melting into the great multitude is another small but recognizable voice—your own! On the day when this vision is reality, you will be standing, *together with the nations*, before the throne in worship!

For years and years, you may have lived as an outsider, apart from the people whom God laid on your heart. So many times, you might have tried to really enter their world, but the walls of culture, language, or distance kept getting in the way. But now, as you stand in his glorious presence, together in worship, we are one body, one bride. There is no longer any dividing wall.

On this great day, we will worship together. We will stand, together with those for whom we have wept, wearing robes made white in the blood of the Lamb.

But slowly, the press of today brings us back to the here and now. Living in time makes it difficult to continually risk it all for eternity. This world can be a rough place for a supernatural vision to survive. For this reason, we occasionally need to hear the sounds of such heavenly worship. It helps our inner man keep his bearings through this fleeting vapor we call a lifetime. So go ahead, just stop and listen for a while.

The Lord Determines Our Steps

In their hearts humans plan their course,
but the LORD establishes their steps.
—Proverbs 16:9

How many times have I "planned my course" only to have an unseen hand change the rules of the game!

Despite knowing better, how often do I attempt to take hold of my own destiny, calculating the best way this one life will be spent? A few years preparing for this, a decade or two doing that, maybe a couple of months sick leave—just in case. But as surely as summer follows spring, the master of my fate asserts his will at a time of his own choosing. Then, everything I have so carefully calculated is thrown into chaos, and my little chess pieces lie scattered all over the floor.

Usually, this is the point when frustration begins to smolder and the dark smell of despair starts to hang over my thought life. My emotions commence swinging wildly, one minute dragging me about as a weary slave in chains and the next demanding to reinstall self on the throne. If you see in this picture a portrait of yourself as well, take heart. In these words from the wise son of King David, we are saved from such wasted emotional debauchery.

The verse begins by affirming our normal human desire to have a course, to have purpose. We should take courage in the fact that Scripture considers it proper for us to set a plan for ourselves and live by it. At times it may need correcting. Occasionally, it may even need a complete revision; nevertheless, we have purpose.

As we meditate on this truth, the soul slowly becomes aware of the second anchor point found in the next line. Not only am I to be a person with deep purpose, but I am also one whose steps are directed. There really is someone in charge, and thankfully I am not he.

My life sometimes feels like a swirling chaos; I cannot understand why this thing happened or that thing did not. But over the years, I am learning that I have no need to resist the one who choreographs my steps. I can have confidence in his unseen hand. Often, I don't understand his reasons, but I must trust his heart toward me.

Jesus said that we would be his witnesses.

This is essential to the missions heart. Why? Because Jesus said that we would *be* his witnesses. He did not say that we would go about "witnessing," simply making an announcement of his message, using whatever means are most advantageous. Like it or not, our lives are the window through which the gospel is understood. The way we walk out our faith is an oft-read commentary on the meaning of this great salvation. If we wish to convincingly proclaim that there is a loving, all-wise Lord who transcends history, then we must live as though that were true. Our lives must show a skeptical world that we do not believe ourselves to be in control, but neither do we live as helpless pawns of fate.

Everything about our way of life must speak of an interactive relationship with this eternal King we claim to know. Sometimes, he directs us *through* the desires of our heart. Other times, he directs *in spite of* those desires. A dynamic tension exists. We have purpose, yet we do not control how that purpose plays out. We act in faith yet remain yielded to an unseen hand. This is not an easy way to live, but when we do so, it presents a powerful witness. Our friends and neighbors, whether in Seattle or Singapore, must see us living comfortably within this paradox because it is a message the world needs to see in order to believe.

Against All Hope

Against all hope,
Abraham in hope believed and so became
the father of many nations, just as it had been said to him,
"So shall your offspring be."
—Romans 4:18

What had been twenty-five years of pain and emotional turmoil for Abraham is easily stated in a brief verse—only twenty-eight words. What would have been agony to live through becomes hardly an afterthought when viewed from the hindsight of the passing of centuries.

Those years he and Sarah waited for their promised son must have been filled with unbelievable doubt and anxiety. Genesis tells us a great deal about that time in their lives, but the name Ishmael sums it up quite nicely. Every time this cute little boy tugged at his father's sleeve calling "Papa, Papa," it was a reminder to the couple of their spiritual impotence. Their failure, and its cost to their entire family, paints as bleak a picture as any found in Scripture.

Yet, the vantage point of many centuries later provides us a wider perspective on their struggle of faith. It is also the only hope for us to understand the purposes of God in our own lives. For no matter how strong we think we are, no matter how solid our convictions, our humanity seems to always keep us from seeing the grand design of God. But thankfully, that does not stop him from accomplishing his purposes.

A wonderful example is seen in the life of Saint Patrick of Ireland. Few realize that he was British, a young man whose first taste of Irish hospitality came during the years spent as a slave. Yet such bitterness was an eternal handmaiden for revealing the purpose and plan of God. His hardships were part of what enabled Patrick to hear and respond to a calling to reach the Irish people. His story is but one in a vast gallery of lives that were impossible to understand in their day of trouble but shine like a beacon to us now.

Many, if not most, of these saints died without seeing the fruit their dreams would someday bear.

David Livingstone died in faith, believing for the countless African churches of today. William Carey poured out his life for an India that is now sending out missionaries of her own. These and countless others lived, toiled, and died by faith. They did not know the outcome of their personal stories during the dark, painful years of waiting and trial. Many, if not most, of these saints died without seeing the fruit their dreams would someday bear. Like Abraham before them, literally decades of their lives could be told in twenty-eight words or less.

The painful truth is that few of us are adept at foreseeing the future. We are usually blinded by the here and now. Even in that, we seldom see the hand of God in our present circumstances because of our many fears and insecurities. It is simply an unfortunate part of our humanity that we often lose sight of God's purposes in our lives—shortsightedness seems to come to us by nature.

Yet, this should not discourage us. For the proof of a divine, unseen hand is not an invincible human will. Rather, the evidence of such things is written only in retrospect. It is only future generations who will be able to read such stories about us.

31 A Man of Unclean Lips

"Woe to me!" I cried.
"I am ruined! For I am a man of unclean lips,
and I live among a people of unclean lips,
and my eyes have seen the King, the LORD Almighty." . . .
Then I heard the voice of the Lord saying,
"Whom shall I send? And who will go for us?
—Isaiah 6:5, 8

The words of verses five and eight are inseparably linked; we can't understand one without the other. There is an intimate connection between the "undoneness" Isaiah felt in the presence of the Lord and his receptivity to the call a few moments later. A true vision of God will change a person. God is an all-consuming fire that leaves no one the same. It is just such a vision of the Almighty that gives a person the power to spend the rest of his life preaching to hard, religious people or, like Isaiah, to die a horrible death at the hands of those to whom he was sent.

It is one thing for a person to hear *about* the Lord; this may or may not have an effect on him. But it is another matter altogether for one to come into the presence of this awesome King. It is impossible to be the same afterward. This is what happened to Isaiah. He had a direct encounter with a holy God, and it wounded him. The sight of true holiness uncovered all his unrighteousness and prepared his heart to hear words that would forever change the direction of his life.

Many know about God. This is a great problem in the increasingly post-Christian West. Such people are all around us. They sell us shoes; they sell us abortions. They fill pulpits and pews; they fill their pockets; they might even fill slots on missions boards. To only know *about* God is dangerous. It makes a person full of religion yet leaves them lacking the Spirit whose yearnings words cannot fully express.

Fulfilling the Great Commission will not be completed by such as these. No, it is not their birthright. This glorious mission requires people who live on a much more intimate basis with this God they claim to represent. But be forewarned, such intimacy will undo us, just as it did Isaiah.

Those who have thus encountered the living Lord
never live the same afterward;
it changes them.

Yet, it is hard for us to admit that our foolish human pride needs to be undone, to be ruined, from time to time. But ruined it must be. It helps us keep a clarity about our calling. We must be reminded that we are not a part of Christ's Great Commission because of our goodness but rather despite our lack of it.

Those who have thus encountered the living Lord never live the same afterward; it changes them. And this is precisely why we go. This is why we give. This is why we pray. This is why we keep on going and giving and praying with a passion that defies sound reason.

I can imagine Isaiah reflecting on his encounter with the Lord in the hard times. It would have been a source of strength to him, for in it he not only saw his own sinfulness, but he saw the one who called him in all his awesome splendor. And *that* vision was far more powerful than the ugliness of life that surrounded him.

The mission challenges that face the church today are much like those that Isaiah faced. Often, we are called to speak to the same kind of hard, religious people. The world around us is full of them—the Hindu has millions of gods, the Muslim has one angry one, and the materialist has one carried in a wallet. These people don't need more religion; they already have far too much. Some of them have so much religion that they just might kill you because of it—as they did Isaiah. The only person who can honestly face such a reality is one who has had a personal power encounter with a holy God and spontaneously replied—"Here am I. Send me."

Our Witness to the Next Generation

One generation commends your works to another;
they tell of your mighty acts. They tell of the power
of your awesome works—and I will proclaim your great deeds.
They celebrate your abundant goodness
and joyfully sing of your righteousness
—Psalm 145:4, 6–7

What will our generation commend to the next? Will we speak of the wonders of our technology and advances in medicine? Will we praise the ease and comfort of international travel and its effect on world missions? Or will we proclaim the power of God's awesome works and celebrate his abundant goodness?

In one short generation, we went from rejoicing over scratchy gospel recordings in a few tribal languages to a digitally mastered *Jesus* film on multilingual flash drives. We have gone from marveling at an occasional international telephone call to 24/7 internet access with video calls.

Technology is now playing an enormous role in the life of the missions heart. Therefore, it is easy to fall into a trap, leaving our love for gadgets as our main legacy. It is true that God has graciously given us incredible new tools for the task, but they are not what deserves remembrance. Just as people merit no praise when the God of glory chooses to work through them, neither should we leave behind a fascination with the paraphernalia that each generation carries into the task.

What we should truly marvel at is that God's redemptive story is now being played out among new peoples and nations, among those who have never heard before. Technology may have played a part in that story, but we must be careful, lest we give the impression that it was the driving factor.

What we should truly marvel at
is that God's redemptive story is now being played out
among new peoples and nations,
among those who have never heard before.

But if we are honest with ourselves, this will be hard for our generation. We are slowly becoming more and more intertwined with the hidden technology we now depend on. It is much more difficult for us to see the quiet and mysterious hand of God working behind the scenes when we are bombarded by emails and cellphone calls.

Therefore, our testimony on this issue must be deliberate. We must say, loudly and repeatedly, that the unreached nations are being discipled because of God's "abundant goodness" and "mighty acts," not because of our great advances in technology.

If we do not, those in the future will have a distorted picture of who, or what, was responsible for the great advance in world missions that is happening in our time.

And this rate of change is ever accelerating; the next generation will have even better tools at their disposal than the ones we have used. It is for this reason imperative that we pass along to them something more than a fascination with our electronic toys. We must entrust them with the clear understanding that it is God, and him alone, who deserves the glory. We must model to them a silent awe of the majestic power and great deeds of the Lord. And we must make it clear that these great acts of his mercy stand above and beyond the stream of progress that we have been riding.

Our testimony in this is very important. We not only have a responsibility to testify to the lost, but we also have an obligation to show the way for those who will follow us in this great relay race we call world missions. If we don't point them to the greatness of our God, who are we expecting will do it?

David Sought the Lord

David and his men wept aloud
until they had no strength left to weep. …
David was greatly distressed
because the men were talking of stoning him.
… But David found strength in the LORD his God.
—1 Samuel 30:4, 6

Here, we see David enduring one of those great trials that tested him during the days before the kingdom became his own. While he and his men were away at war, an Amalekite raiding party swooped in and carried away everything in David's camp—the wives of all the men, all their children, and all their goods. Everything was gone, including David's own family. For most of us, a tragedy of this magnitude is beyond comprehension, a profound picture of desolation and pain.

If we are honest, we will admit at least a little empathy with the men's urge to vent their pain on someone, anyone—perhaps especially toward David. He was, after all, the leader of this motley crew. At times, he even sounded like a prophet. Could he not have somehow foreseen the tragedy and prevented it?

But rather than reviewing emotions we can easily understand, I want to examine something that is much more difficult to grasp, the remarkable steadfastness of David. Here, facing this most bitter experience, yet another in long years of bitterness, David again did as he had always done—he turned to the Lord his God.

He knew exactly where to go when the word *bleak* was overly optimistic. Do we? What do we do when the enemy is raiding our camp and hope has vanished as the morning mist? I fear that we do not always respond as David did, but more often like the rest of the men. We rant and rave, looking for someone to stone.

The revelation of David's true character is seen in the fact that he could seek the Lord even when it appeared that God had abandoned him.

Yet here, we see David somehow finding strength in the Lord. Despite overwhelming personal grief and pain, he sought his God. He did not forget the Rock to whom he could run in times of trouble. Could this be why David is remembered more for his heart than for his sins, although both are plainly recorded in Scripture? Could this be the quality that caused an insignificant Middle Eastern shepherd to soar out of the pages of history and become an example of pure worship for future generations of believers?

David was a man who sought the Lord.

With the hindsight of passing centuries, we can see that this moment represents a turning point in David's story. Shortly after this dark and dreadful day, God delivered all their families, unharmed, back to David and his men. And soon after that, the Lord gave the kingdom to David as well. But remember, the soon-to-be king could not read ahead as we often do. He knew none of these wonderful things as he groped through that day's pain to find his God.

The revelation of David's true character is seen in the fact that he could seek the Lord even when it appeared that God had abandoned him. This was the measure of his spirituality and leadership. His men needed someone to show the way out of the pit of despair they were in. They needed a real, a spiritual leader.

Whether our leadership is expressed in the pulpit, a prayer group, a mission, or primarily in our own family, those around us need to be pointed to God when times are dark and hopeless. Someone must lead the way. This is not hard to do when all is well and compliments are dropping in our laps like money from heaven. But what of the days when the sun will not shine and the heavens are brass? How do we respond when things look like they did for David that day, a flood of evil quickly going from bad to worse? Do we steadfastly seek God in these awful times or only when prayer is easy and worship a joy?

These are hard questions, but they are the measure of our true spirituality. A leader is not always the one with the title, nor the one receiving all the accolades. At the end of the day, the one who leads is the one who seeks the Lord.

Authority Rooted in Love

Although in Christ I could be bold and order you
to do what you ought to do,
yet I prefer to appeal to you on the basis of love.
—Philemon 8–9

As it concerns the real world in which most missionaries live, these are some of the most practical yet profound words ever penned by the apostle Paul.

By this time, the great missionary evangelist was an old man, his body marked by the scars of many beatings. His gray hair and many sufferings for the sake of the gospel had given him a mark of authority that was beginning to be honored across the wider church. In large part due to his efforts, this young church now stretched all the way around the Mediterranean basin.

Yet when it came to exercising his spiritual authority, he was humble and preferred an appeal to love rather than to the clout that he had earned. Let us review the details found in Philemon. Here is a short personal letter, the main thrust of which is Paul asking a brother named Philemon to forgive a runaway slave named Onesimus. Most likely, the occasion for the letter was that Paul was making the new believer, Onesimus, return to his master. But at the same time, he was asking the master, a fellow lover of Christ, to be forgiving.

It does not take a degree in New Testament history to guess that this is not the way conflicts between slave and masters usually worked out in the first-century world. Paul knew that Philemon would probably want his returning slave whipped—or worse. Slavery is an ugly institution that taints all involved, even otherwise godly people. But what is more important to us is that Paul also knew that as an apostle he could act decisively to stop this. It was his right to act with strong spiritual authority. He says this clearly, "In Christ I could be bold and order you . . ." Indeed, some might even say it was Paul's moral responsibility to stop any harm from coming to the returning runaway. But for some reason, the apostle stopped short of making demands of Philemon. This may, at first, seem hard to understand, but understand we must because there is something important going on here.

We too have real kingdom authority—it is the King who has sent us—and we have a responsibility to use this spiritual authority properly. But we should take a lesson from Paul here and realize that obedience that is forced or demanded is not what God's kingdom is about. The real measure of spiritual authority is not how many we can force to obey us, but rather how many willingly follow our leadership and submit to our authority.

We too have real kingdom authority—
it is the King who has sent us—and we have a
responsibility to use this spiritual authority properly.

Certainly, there are times when the missionary must use her spiritual authority to protect the interests of the weak and oppressed; this is good and right. But I fear that we often go so far beyond this mandate that we have lost our way. If you doubt, look at the way many Western missionaries relate to their local brothers and sisters. It looks more like an employer-employee model than the wise elder brother we see in Paul's appeal to Philemon.

Unlike Paul, we quickly command people to "do what they ought to do" as Paul could have, when we should be appealing for them to follow our lead on the basis of built-up trust and love. Perhaps we use our authority or force of personality to coerce others because it is easier than setting an example of leadership that they would follow willingly.

It seems that Paul had in mind something greater than the safety of Onesimus, even though that would have been a worthy cause. Paul was after Philemon's heart. He wanted to turn it toward Onesimus. He wanted to see an offended Christian brother receive and forgive the offending party, a powerful display of grace in a realm that knew little about mercy. This witness to the ugly world of slavery was so important that Paul was willing to set aside his God-given authority and trust the work of the Holy Spirit in Philemon's heart. Now that is apostolic faith!

May God grant us the same grace so that we use our authority in ways that honor the Spirit's work in other people's hearts.

To Him Who Is Able

Now to him who is able to do
immeasurably more than all we ask or imagine,
according to his power that is at work within us,
to him be glory in the church and in Christ Jesus
throughout all generations, for ever and ever! Amen.
—Ephesians 3:20–21

How the missions heart needs to feed on this verse! In a way perhaps unique to the task of global evangelization, we need to know that we appeal to someone who is "able to do immeasurably more than all we can ask or imagine."

Notice that Paul did not write that God is able to do "more" than we ask, but "immeasurably more," "exceedingly more," "infinitely more"—depending on your translator's pick of superlatives.

Imagine a book compiling every request that has been made at all the prayer meetings you have ever attended—he is able to do more. Add to that the countless prayer letters and emails that you have either written or received—he is still able. Top this off with the secret longings of your heart, the things that you scarcely dare to dream because you could never expect them to be answered. Even the sum of all these burdens and dreams for the nations do not represent the slightest challenge to our God!

Like a slow sunrise, I am starting to believe the truth that our God is not limited. This has not been easy.

The awareness that comes with a life in missions keeps getting in the way. Huge, global needs and mega-crises in the daily news quickly beat me down.

It seems that almost daily, a lying little demon who claims to be reality stands behind me recounting the ugly, grim details. This hateful companion mocks my heart any time I dare to believe God for more. The results are often predictable—I end up praying for only what I think God could do if he were puny and limited like me. I stop daring to dream of what God will do since he is God.

But the missions heart must rise to the occasion; acting in faith is imperative. There is no substitute for a person who knows the true source of power, for God is not working out there somewhere. Paul says this exceedingly great power is "at work within us."

Selah. Allow just a moment for that to sink in.

We must remember that the power of God, which is infinitely beyond our imagination, surges through our hearts when we pray.

This God of ours, whose power is without compare, has chosen to express his power through us—flawed, even broken, vessels. Why? We will never understand. We can only kneel in awe of this God who allows us to represent his kingdom on the earth.

Of course, it would be less painful for us if God would just go out and do whatever he wanted, without our involvement. But this is not his way. He has bottled up his great self in simple human hearts. Therefore, as his servants in a great cause, we must stop limiting God by our small imaginations. We must remember that the power of God, which is infinitely beyond our imagination, surges through our hearts when we pray. It opens infinite possibilities whenever we speak the name of Jesus in dark and desolate spiritual places.

If I am honest, this truth is too wonderful for me. Nevertheless, I embrace it. I embrace it because the missions heart cannot live long without it, and it is our great hope for reaching the nations.

In What Do You Delight?

Blessed is the one . . . whose delight is in the law of the LORD,
and who meditates on his law day and night.
That person is like a tree planted by streams of water,
which yields its fruit in season and whose leaf does not wither—
whatever they do prospers.
—Psalm 1:1–3

In this first of the Psalms, David described the natural result of a life that is God oriented. Like an illustrator who brings sketches to life with touches of color, David painted light strokes of flesh and blood on the idea of what it means to be "blessed." The result is a beautiful picture, but one that uses imagery with which we may be unfamiliar. Therefore, it would pay good dividends for us to consider these verses for a few moments.

The core of David's illustration is a strong, healthy tree. It fills our mind's eye with images of a sturdy trunk upholding well-shaped branches full of rich fruit—perhaps figs or pears—peeking out of dense foliage.

But this psalm is not about a tree growing to all its lush potential. And it is not really about fruit either. It *is* about location: "He is like a tree planted . . ."

This psalm is about the person who continually places their soul near "streams of water." This matter of location is, in fact, the key to understanding the psalm.

The tree David described is one whose "leaf does not wither," an indication of the continuous spiritual health that awaits those who choose to stay near their God. Since this tree is "planted" in the proper place, in the natural rhythms of life it will bring about fruit—"in season," as David called it.

Now it should be remembered that such a tree may not produce as much fruit as we think we deserve, or even as often as others may expect, but the fruit that it does produce will be real. This is not some kind of genetically engineered super-tree that produces huge crops of tasteless fruit. No, David was contemplating a normal, healthy spiritual life that naturally produces fruit, the kind that is consistent with the flow of the seasons of the soul.

David understood
what many seem to have forgotten today.

Many Christians today are earnestly searching for a new key for their ministry, something to unlock greater fruitfulness in their lives. Unfortunately, others respond to this hunger by peddling their specific methods, promising larger crops and greater fruitfulness if we simply follow their particular rearrangements of the basics.

But we must remember that the spiritual gardener of David's day had no access to the conferences and the turbo-charged resources that now saturate Western Christianity. He worked with simple trees, not modern hybrids. He counted on the reality of the changing seasons, not climate-controlled hothouses. In fact, I believe we can confidently say that the tree David had in mind was not of any special variety at all. It was not intrinsically better than any others. It did not have a bigger, better "calling" than the other trees in the garden. No, the only reason the tree he described was prospering was because of its location.

David understood what many seem to have forgotten today. He knew that a tree's fruitfulness is the direct result of cultivation, and the most important part of that labor of love is location. The tree in the psalmist's picture was bearing fruit as the natural outcome of a location near a faithful water source. The position of our soul near the source of all life is the only trustworthy key to unlock the life and ministry we desire.

This spiritual posture near God is what leads us into a natural, long-lasting fruitfulness—something popular brands of spiritual engineering cannot. Our lives will bear the natural outcome of being rooted in our God and his word. When we delight ourselves in his word and meditate day and night on it, we become planted so closely to the life-giving water that we become the epitome of spiritual health. Such a soul cannot help but bear good fruit.

While this simple truth may not pack conference halls or sell tape series, it *will* bring about the blessed and fruitful life we desire, and that should satisfy the gardener in us all.

A Ring for My Ear

But if your servant [slave] says to you,
"I do not want to leave you,"
because he loves you and your family and is well off with you,
then take an awl and push it through his earlobe into the door,
and he will become your servant [slave] for life.
—Deuteronomy 15:16–17

Slave is an extremely negative word these days, so much so that newer translations of the Bible steer clear of it. But the refinement of modern culture cannot change the raw imagery of this word, which is used repeatedly in Scripture.

Chains. Slave markets. Bondage of body and mind. The slave is a person whose will has been stripped away. Their vocabulary has lost the word *no*, for they are subject to the absolute power of another. To children of the Enlightenment and civil rights, this is a repulsive thought. It is certainly not an attractive picture to paint as a similitude of Christian devotion. Yet it is an astoundingly accurate one—with one modifier—ours is a willing servitude.

The passage above tells of such a strange, almost absurd paradox—a willing slave. A Hebrew slave was one of a proud race who, because of some profound misfortune, was forced to sell himself into slavery. This was a person whose life had become so destitute that only by an act of another could they be redeemed back to wholeness.

But then the picture sharpens. After the debt has been cleared, after wholeness has been restored, they decide in effect to sell themselves again. But this time, it is not out of poverty or need but for love of their master.

Here, we see someone who in the past has served out of debt and fear, but from this day forward will serve out of devotion. By the law, the debt was paid—freedom was their right. Yet this person chose to stay enslaved because of a bond to their master that was stronger than any chain. Something had occurred on a deeper level. A new form of relationship had been forged between master and slave—one of trust.

This is the place of maturity in ministry.

The relationship changed because they had come to trust their master's good intentions toward them. They had seen his character over the years and now knew that only good would come to them from serving out their days in his house. In fact, such a life of servitude was preferable to freedom precisely for this reason—in the master's will there was nothing to fear. The master's heart had been revealed, and its beauty drew the slave like a magnet. How could someone not want to spend the rest of their life in the shelter of such a good and benevolent will?

The slave is now free, in a sense, to obey whatever the master bids them because they understand that come what may, the master's intentions toward them are perpetually and profoundly good. This conviction then births a turning point in the relationship that is marked by a hole in the slave's ear as a symbol of a permanent yet free willingness to listen to the master's voice.

Ah, here is the rub of the story and its bite into our lives. It is one thing to heed Christ's call to the nations because we feel some sort of debt or fear, but do we freely give ourselves to obedience? Have we really come to trust the goodness of our Master's will?

Our ministry and service in the kingdom can be done out of a sense of duty and obligation. In this way, many missions hearts offer a labor of drudgery. But the Master bids us to cross the threshold into his house willingly, as a slave who has come to trust him and his good intentions toward us.

And once we do, this trust flows two ways. Once our servitude becomes a free release of our will, our Master can entrust us with greater responsibilities because his love, which redeemed us out of our poverty, has now been reciprocated. He knows that our bond is no longer according to the law but that of a joyful heart.

This is the place of maturity in ministry. It is when we know that we are free to turn away, even run, yet we willingly remain bound to his will. Such a slave is forever marked—by an ear open to the Master's voice.

When We Lack Wisdom

If any of you lacks wisdom, you should ask God, who gives generously to all without finding fault, and it will be given to you.
—James 1:5

Sometimes I think that this verse was written specifically for those pursuing God's heart for the nations. "If any of you lacks wisdom . . ." The missions heart often wonders, "When was it that I *did not* lack enough wisdom for this calling?"

As those who seek to fulfill the Great Commission, the task before us is great, and its complications are innumerable. Often, we feel so completely "over our heads" that we wonder why we have not yet drowned? The matters demanding divine wisdom are many.

Wisdom to know how to bear a meaningful and true witness of Jesus in cultures different from our own. Wisdom to know how to use our financial resources to bless, without leaving behind dependency as a curse. Wisdom to balance life, ministry, family, and personal devotion.

The list is long. No matter what your role in this great enterprise, a defining part of it is the need for wisdom. Therefore, we can take great comfort in these words from James, the brother of our Lord. We each face, in differing ways, so many obstacles and complex situations. Yet, here we are offered a straightforward means toward answers: Simply ask in faith.

Over the years I have come to rely on this promise like a shipwrecked man relies on his life preserver—I cling to it. It is my only hope of knowing what I should do in so much of my ministry; of that, I am well aware. With a combination of fear and faith, I hold fast to the offer promised through James's words.

As those who seek to fulfill the Great Commission,
the task before us is great,
and its complications are innumerable.

We must start to believe that God will continuously give us the wisdom we need, without reproving us for being so foolish that we need to ask. He does not dispense these fatherly insights grudgingly, as though they were based on our deservedness. Nor is he stingy, as though we might squander any excess we receive from his hand. We must learn to run, with confidence, to a wise and generous God who is quick to share his thoughts with us, not scold us for being ignorant.

This means we must hold a theology which teaches God genuinely delights in sharing his intimate thoughts with us. This is one of those "good and perfect gifts" that James writes of later in his letter. We must think of the wisdom we need as a natural part of our relationship with him and, as with all other good things, something he gives in abundance, far greater than we deserve.

Perhaps one of the difficulties is that many Christians still think like people under the law. We subconsciously believe that God will only give us what we deserve, and we all know how little that should be! Yet how many of the problems we face would be resolved if we truly believed these words of James? How many sleepless nights have been wasted because we have not lived in the light of this promise?

The more we believe this exhortation, the less anxiety we will have as we go about life and ministry. Despite the countless times that personal experience or training provides no guidance to us, we can always trust our gracious God who delights to give the wisdom we need, if only we will ask him.

The Patient Endurance of the Saints

Whoever has ears, let them hear.
"If anyone is to go into captivity, into captivity they will go.
If anyone is to be killed with the sword,
with the sword they will be killed."
—Revelation 13:9–10

Great atrocities are being committed against the people of God. In some places around the globe, your worst nightmares are reality for some of our brothers and sisters. Surely God could deliver them from these horrible situations, could he not? Can it be his will that his people suffer so much?

Of course, God is capable of intervention, but there are times when he chooses not to. This is hard for us to understand, but in the economy of God, the circumstances of our lives don't merit as much importance as we might like. Rather, it is our *response* to these circumstances that is his concern. For, in our *response* to circumstances, character is forged, and character is the fruit that God is looking for in his vineyard.

Notice, in this passage, there is not even a hint of how our loving heavenly Father feels about these outrages against his beloved ones. No doubt, his great heart is broken by the pain and suffering they at times endure. To be sure, his retribution will be fierce on the day he avenges them. But here, he only addresses what he expects from his children in the midst of these tirades that are rebellion against him and his throne.

Now, all this is fine-sounding theory. It is easy to teach in the classroom or preach from the pulpit. Easy, that is, so long as that classroom or pulpit has not been splattered by the blood of martyrs. Once that dark specter has entered our lives, or the lives of those to whom we are sent, our classroom theology rings hollow.

For the missions heart, all too often these previously abstract concepts turn into searing pain and tears. Easy answers die young in such company, and it becomes impossible to just read over such words and go on as if nothing happened.

This requires a kind of faith that is not in vogue today—a faith that is a strong statement about God, his sovereignty, and our submission to him.

How then do we continue to believe these words are from God yet keep ourselves from a cold distancing of the heart? How can we see the evil in pain and suffering yet not lose our faith in the goodness of God?

This requires a kind of faith that is not in vogue today—a faith that is a strong statement about God, his sovereignty, and our submission to him. It requires of us a faith that can understand our own insignificance yet balance it with our being an important part of God's redemptive purposes in the earth.

Perhaps it will help us to think of our lives as one small thread woven into a much larger tapestry. God is not oblivious to the suffering of his loved ones, and he will avenge. But for now, he requires that we offer our faithfulness as simple acts of devotion amid pain. In so doing, we add a few strands of color to the whole.

This is not a fatalistic theology; rather, it is the call to an aggressive abandonment to the hand of a heavenly Father in whom we trust. It is the fruit of the deep working of the Spirit through which we can give ourselves to this "patient endurance and faithfulness on the part of God's people." And this is how we add our small testimony to a faith that is stronger than blind hatred and greater than the grave.

Following the Path of the Righteous

The path of the righteous is like the morning sun, shining ever brighter till the full light of day.
—Proverbs 4:18

What does the mysterious thing we call guidance from the Lord look like in real life? This proverb may be as close to an answer as we will ever find in Scripture. This is because his word into the human heart is not some set regimen with its own rules and regulations. In fact, I dare say that no two of the Lord's servants are likely to perceive his guidance in exactly the same way.

Rather, it starts like a faint glow in the eastern sky, sometimes pink, sometimes orange—other times it is a color whose name only the angels know. At first, it is almost imperceptible, but to the one who is acquainted with the quiet of the early morning hours, the signs are clear: The morning has come. We know that everything will soon be clear because he is beginning to show his hand.

But even to the experienced soul, this hour is a difficult time. One must fumble and feel her way about. We may be sure the Master is speaking, even how we should respond, but my, how dark is the path on which he leads! Fear and doubt, faith and excitement, all run together as our eyes scan the distance, trying desperately to adjust to the genesis of a new day. Nothing is clear in our line of sight, except that to turn back would be worse than whatever lies ahead.

As fearsome as this moment can be, it is the beginning of divine guidance. It is the required place for us to start walking, nervously putting one foot in front of the other. Sometimes with confidence, other times despite ourselves. We hesitate; we stumble. Anxiety rises to meet us, all our fears ruminating together about what may go wrong. But the one who wants to know the joy of being led by the Spirit will press ahead.

In these dimly lit hours, every act is an act of faith, even the small things. To even try to believe that the voice in the distance is the calling of our heavenly Father is hard. The darkness seems more real than the dawn. Yet, the inner man knows that there is too much light to stay in slumber; it is time to obey.

In these dimly lit hours, every act is an act of faith, even the small things.

Then, as we start walking in the twilight, the enemy begins sneering at us. He tries to defame our Father's loving care, his obnoxious innuendo turning every obstacle into a threat. Satan swears that he can see further, that he is wiser, and that to go on will be our undoing because the worst of all fates awaits our next step.

Yet after only a few short moments of obedience, the light comes on stronger. Now the powerful, streaking bolts of our Lord's face begin to blaze across the sky. We quickly see that the lies our enemy was spewing were no more than the sound of him running from the rays of the rising Son!

The things that were so frightening and uncertain a few moments ago become ablaze with the light of his glory. The enemy's voice and his menacing shadows are shown for what they were all along—powerless, hollow threats. Even our greatest fear, the grave, lies defanged in the face of him who is eternal life. Now, with each step, the going gets easier. Not all at once, mind you, but finally we can see the path is real! The Lord really has gone before us and laid out a plan. The longer we walk, the smoother it becomes.

This is the picture of divine guidance, as painted for us in the proverb. It is like a great sign in the sky, rising to meet all those who are willing to step out by faith and meet the dawn.

Closing Thoughts

While writing this devotional, I came across a powerful quote in a now forgotten place. With respect and apologies to the original author, I wish to share it with you: "The work I do is bigger than the person I am."

Barely more than ten words, yet epic in its implications. As I chewed on this little cud, it began to feed my soul. Ever so slowly, it defeated some of the inner fears that warred against me as I tried to share my heart with you in these devotions.

"The work I do is bigger than the person I am."

It relieved a great burden by reminding me that my writing is not limited to who I am. For you see, I am well aware of my own insignificance. I am little more than so much dust on the scales.

I may call myself a missionary, but my name is not worthy to be mentioned in the same breath as people like William Carey, Amy Carmichael, or Jim Elliot—saints whose lives changed the course of history. My own short blossom in the field will never produce anything that could compare with the incredible lasting fruit their lives bore.

However, while I may not personally belong in such company, I bear, in my thinking and writing, their mark on the world. I have been shaped by their examples as to the nature of the missions heart. In a very real way, they taught me. The stories from their lives—their faith and sacrifice—have indelibly imprinted a passion on my heart that I cannot run from. Thought by thought, some of who they are—in the eternal present tense—is being synthesized into the person God is making of me.

Writing this book is one way that I fulfill a calling to continue their legacy. Every time I put pen to page, I draw from a deep well of inspiration that others have dug and unknowingly entrusted to me. And I do this fully aware that any ability I have is God given so that I might pass along the blessing I have received.

But as I write, I am also painfully aware that I do not live up to everything that I draw from that deep well. I write challenging thoughts only because I know how much those thoughts challenged my own soul in the thinking of them. Often, I fall far short of the pictures my words paint. Does that mean I allow myself an excuse to become a hypocrite hiding behind the page?

No. It just means that these devotionals are not limited to what I have been able to live out. While my heart presses me to live more like Jesus tomorrow than I did today, it does not bind my writing to that which I have already attained. Therefore, I do not write as an instructor at the lectern, but rather as a beggar who has found some bread. The excitement in my words is only that of a hungry heart who has the joy of sharing a few precious crumbs. Such precious crumbs they are!

"The work I do is bigger than the person I am."

It is both a statement of present humble truth and a prophecy of who I wish to become.

Other titles you may enjoy ...

When Serving Gets Tough: A Thirty-Day Devotional for Missionaries

Carol Ghattas

Veteran missionary and author Carol Ghattas shares her experiences, providing practical guidance and hope through Scripture for anyone struggling with the demands of cross-cultural service. Each daily entry is designed to help missionaries reconnect with their faith. Ghattas acknowledges that there is no one-size-fits-all solution to ministry trials but emphasizes that there is one God always ready to help and heal. Whether you're facing doubts, loneliness, or exhaustion, this devotional provides a balm for weary souls.

Bags Packed, Hearts Ready: Stories of God's Faithfulness in Cross-Cultural Ministry

Sue Eenigenburg

What happens when the familiar comforts are stripped away, and you're left to confront the raw realities of your calling? In *Bags Packed, Hearts Ready*, Sue Eenigenburg shares heartfelt reflections that delve into her experiences as a cross-cultural worker and mother. Through personal anecdotes, humor, and scriptural insight, she reveals how grace, gratitude, and trust in God can transform even the most challenging times into testimonies of divine provision and strength. Each story in this book ends with questions and a space to reflect and pray.

Sacred Courage: Thinking Biblically About Fear and Anxiety

Betsy Kirk

Fear can find a way into every heart and can shape our lives in unexpected ways. In this book, Betsy Kirk helps Christians fight against fear with faith in God. The author's own battle against fear—from childhood to motherhood, from Minnesota to Indonesia—is woven throughout the book. Each chapter offers fresh meditations on biblical passages to develop a response to fear that is theologically informed. Chapters conclude with discussion questions, challenging readers to examine their own hearts. This book will find a wide audience among those seeking relief from fear and anxiety.

Downward Discipleship: How Amy Carmichael Gave Me Courage to Serve in a Slum

Anita Rahma

Downward Discipleship beckons you to learn from Amy Carmichael's life—her fifty-year mission to rescue temple-bound girls becomes a canvas for seven invitations of discipleship. Rahma weaves in her own stirring narrative from Jakarta's slums, presenting a model of discipleship that is demanding as it is rewarding, challenging as it is inspiring. Rahma points us to a life of downward discipleship—to follow our savior to unlikely places, meet him among the world's poor, and experience the joy of abundant life.

www.ingramcontent.com/pod-product-compliance
Ingram Content Group UK Ltd.
Pitfield, Milton Keynes, MK11 3LW, UK
UKHW042002190726
13854UKWH00005B/2134